101 Things To Do With Chile Peppers

101 Things To Do With Chile Peppers

BY SANDRA HOOPES

GIBBS SMITH
TO ENRICH AND INSPIRE HUMANKIND

First Edition
21 20 19 18 17   5 4 3 2 1

Text © 2017 Sandra Hoopes

101 Things is a registered trademark of Gibbs Smith,
Publisher and Stephanie Ashcraft.

Published by
Gibbs Smith
P.O. Box 667
Layton, Utah 84041

1.800.835.4993 orders
www.gibbs-smith.com

Printed and bound in Korea

Gibbs Smith books are printed on either recycled, 100% post-consumer
waste, FSC-certified papers or on paper produced from sustainable PEFC-
certified forest/controlled wood source. Learn more at www.pefc.org.

Library of Congress Cataloging-in-Publication Data

Names: Hoopes, Sandra, author.
Title: 101 things to do with chile peppers / Sandra Hoopes.
Other titles: One hundred and one things to do with chile peppers
Description: Layton, Utah : Gibbs Smith, [2017]
Identifiers: LCCN 2016033643 | ISBN 9781423644330 (laminated softcover
  wire-bound)
Subjects: LCSH: Cooking (Hot peppers) | LCGFT: Cookbooks.
Classification: LCC TX803.P46 H66 2017 | DDC 641.3/384--dc23
LC record available at https://lccn.loc.gov/2016033643

This book is dedicated to "Chile Lovers" everywhere, and to my husband, my partner, my typist. I am nothing without you.

www.gibbs-smith.com

CONTENTS

Side Dishes

Cheesy Calabacitas 62 • Mexican Street Corn on the Cob 63 • Green Chile Mac 'n' Cheese 64 • Green Chile Potato Gratin 65 • Cheddar-Bacon Grits 66 • Chile Potato Stacks 67 • Hasselback Potatoes Enchilada-Style 68

Salsas and Sauces

Classic Red Chile Mole 70 • Lazy Summer Salsa 72 • Ranchero Sauce 73 • Avocado-Tomatillo Salsa 74 • Salsa Verde 75 • Authentic Red Chile Enchilada Sauce 76 • Southwest Enchilada Sauce 77 • Tomatillo Cream Sauce 78 • Chimichurri Salsa 79 • Mayan-Spiced Mango Sauce 80

Desserts

Peanut Butter Bombs 82 • Aztec Chocolate Cream Pie 83 • Grilled Mango with Honey and Pistachios 84 • Fiery Chocolate-Dipped Strawberries 85 • Mexican Rocky Road Ice Cream 86 • Spicy Candied Nuts 87 • Raspberry Red Chile Sorbet 88 • Green Chile Apple Crostata 89 • Mexican Chocolate Brownies 90 • Mayan Truffles 91 • Churros with Chile Sugar 92 • Mexican Chocolate-Walnut Fudge 93 • Mayan Chocolate Ganache 94 • Mexican Chocolate-Pecan Cake 95 • Orange Polenta Cake 96 • Orange-Habanero Glaze 97 • Raspberry-Chipotle Donut Bites 98 • Strawberry Limeade Popsicles 99 • Flourless Chocolate-Chile Cake 100 • Mango-Habanero Popsicles 102 • Orange-Habanero Creme Brulee 103

Beverages, Condiments, and Garnishes

Chile Lemonade 106 • Mexican Hot Chocolate 107 • Cafe Ole (Coffee with Mexican Chocolate) 108 • El Toreador Mocktail 109 • Bloody Maria Mocktail 110 • Mango-Habanero Liquado 111 • Cherry Bomb Limeade 112 • Chile-Lime Vinaigrette 113 • Graham Cracker–Pecan Pie Crust 114 • Candied Jalapenos 115 • Tres Chiles Spice Rub 116 • Chipotle Sour Cream 117 • Green Chile Pesto 118 • Oaxacan Peanuts 119 • Chipotle Mayonnaise 120 • Garlic-Chile Oil 121 • Raspberry-Chipotle Jam 123 • Jalapeno-Orange Vinaigrette 124

HELPFUL HINTS

1. When choosing the perfect chile for your recipe, you will want to consider size, color, and especially the heat of each chile. The heat of a chile is rated based on a Scoville scale that provides a method for measuring the capsaicin, the heat-producing chemical found in chiles. Some of the more common chiles found in local markets, and used in these recipes, and their Scoville heat units (SHU) ranking are as follows (the larger the ranking number, the hotter the chile):

Aji Amarillo (30,000 to 50,000) Bright-yellow chile, about 5–6 inches long. Great for roasting and using in sauces.

Anaheim (500 to 2,500) Bright-green chile, about 6–10 inches long. This chile has a fresh grassy flavor and is excellent for roasting and stuffing.

Ancho (1,000 to 2,000) A poblano that has ripened to red before being dried. This chile has a raisin-like flavor and is one of the three main chiles used in mole.

Cayenne (30,000 to 50,000) Slender, red or green chile, about 2–3 inches long. Generally used in dried powder form.

Chile de arbol (50,000 to 65,000) Small dried chile, about 1–2 inches long. Great for sauces or braising meat and is excellent for grinding into powder and adding to spice mixes.

Chipotle (2,500 to 8,000) A jalapeno that has been smoked and dried. Chipotles can be purchased canned and ready to use in a flavorful adobo sauce.

Fresno (2,500 to 10,000) Similar to a jalapeno in size and shape, this chile turns red as it matures and gets hotter as it ripens.

Guajillo (2,500 to 5,000) Dried, reddish-brown chile, about 3–4 inches long. This chile has a complex flavor with a sweet heat that is perfect for soups, stews, and mole.

Habanero (100,000 to 350,000) Bright-orange chile, about 1–2 inches long. Habaneros have a fruity flavor that goes well with pork, fruit, and desserts.

Hatch (5,000 to 6,000) Bright-green chile, about 6–10 inches long. Similar to an Anaheim chile but grown in Hatch, New Mexico.

Jalapeno (2,500 to 8,000) Green chile, about 2–4 inches long. Arguably the most popular chile in the world, this versatile chile can be roasted, fried, or stuffed.

Mulato (2,500 to 3,000) Dried poblano that has been allowed to fully ripen, making its flavor more complex than an ancho. This is one of the three main chiles used in mole.

Pasilla (1,000 to 2,000) Long, thin chile that turns brown as it ripens, about 6–9 inches long. This dried chile is nicknamed the "little raisin" and is one of the three main chiles used in mole.

Poblano (1,000 to 2,000) Dark-green chile, about 4–5 inches long. Perfect for roasting and stuffing.

Serrano (5,000 to 23,000) Green or red chile, about 1–3 inches long. Looks like a smaller, thinner version of a jalapeno but is much hotter.

2. How to Roast Fresh Chiles

- Buy fresh chiles that are firm, without brown spots, wrinkles, or loose skin.

- Roast chiles outdoors over a wood, charcoal, or gas grill on high heat, or indoors over a gas burner or under the broiler. Cook until skins are charred and blistered on all sides.

- Remove skins by placing roasted chiles in a heatproof bowl covered tightly with plastic wrap to help create steam, which makes it easier to separate skins from the chiles. Remove blackened skins when chiles are cool enough to handle.

- The heat from chiles may be reduced by removing the seeds and ribs, where most of the heat resides.

- Roasted chiles may be frozen with or without skins. Place roasted chiles on a baking sheet that will fit in your freezer and freeze individually. Place frozen chiles in a ziplock bag for easy storage.

3. How to Use Dried Chiles

- Buy unbroken, whole chiles that are evenly dried with no spots or discolorations. Chiles should be supple and somewhat flexible.

- Remove stem and seed bulb from each chile then shake out the seeds. Make a long cut down one side to open chile so it will lie flat. Scrape out remaining seeds and dried ribs.

- Toast chiles in a dry, hot frying pan or griddle, turning often to prevent burning. Toast until fragrant and deeper in color.

- Do not use any burnt chiles; their flavor will ruin the dish.

- Place toasted chiles in a bowl and cover with simmering water. Soak for 20–25 minutes, or until soft. Remove from water and pat dry.

- Rehydrated chiles may be pureed. Remove chiles from water, roughly chop, and place in a blender or food processor with a few spoonfuls of the chile soaking water. Blend to desired consistency.

- Reserve chile water to use in recipes if it has a good flavor and is not bitter.

4. How to Make Chile Powder

- Clean whole dried chiles with a dry cloth.

- Remove stem and seed bulb from each chile. Make a long cut down one side to open the chile so it will lie flat. Remove dried ribs and set aside seeds. Chop chiles into large pieces.

- Toast chiles with seeds in a dry frying pan over low heat until fragrant. Be careful not to burn chiles or seeds. Remove from heat and set aside to cool. Discard any burnt chiles or seeds.

- Place small batches of cool, dry chile pieces and seeds in a spice grinder or blender and grind into a fine powder. Chiles should be dry enough that they do not make a paste. Store chile powder in an airtight container.

- For a complex chile flavor, grind several different chiles together.

5. Feeling the burn from chiles may make you grab for a glass of water, but you can put out the flames much faster with a glass of milk, sour cream, or other fatty dairy products that will create a barrier between your tongue and the heat from the chile. You can also take a bite of bread or flour tortilla and keep it pressed against your tongue to absorb the heat.

6. When working with chiles, always be sure to wear rubber gloves, and do not touch your face, eyes, or any other sensitive areas to prevent burning.

BREAKFAST

HUEVOS EL DIABLO (THE DEVIL'S EGGS)

1–2 links	**Italian sausage,** casings removed
2 tablespoons	**vegetable oil**
1	**small yellow onion,** finely diced
3	**Anaheim chiles,** seeded, finely diced
6 cloves	**garlic,** peeled, minced, divided
½ teaspoon	**cumin**
6	**large tomatoes,** diced
½ cup	**red chile sauce**
	salt and pepper, to taste
6	**eggs**
½ cup	**sour cream**
1	**ripe avocado,** sliced
½ cup	**minced fresh cilantro**

In a large frying pan over medium-high heat, break up and brown the sausage in oil until thoroughly cooked. Remove from pan and drain on a paper towel. Wipe oil from pan and return to heat. Add onion and chiles, and saute until softened, about 5 minutes. Add garlic and cumin, stir, and cook for 2–3 minutes. Add tomatoes and chile sauce, smashing the tomatoes with the back of a spoon. Return sausage to the pan and bring to a boil. Reduce heat to medium-low and simmer until slightly thickened, about 2–4 minutes. Season with salt and pepper.

Make 6 indentations in the tomato sauce for the eggs. Crack eggs one at a time and slide into an indentation. Cover pan and let eggs poach until the whites are set and yolks are runny, about 3–4 minutes. Do not overcook eggs. Eggs will continue to cook when removed from heat, sitting in the warm sauce. Garnish with sour cream, avocado, and cilantro. Makes 6 servings.

SOUFFLED CHILE-CHEESE OMELET

3	**eggs,** separated
I pinch	**salt and pepper**
¼ cup	**grated cheddar or Monterey Jack cheese**
½ ounce	**creamy goat cheese,** crumbled
¼ cup	**diced roasted green chiles**
I tablespoon	**butter or margarine**
½ tablespoon	**vegetable oil**
I recipe	**Salsa Verde** (page 75)
	sour cream

Preheat oven to 375 degrees.

In a medium bowl, whisk egg whites to medium peaks. In a separate bowl, mix together the egg yolks, salt, and pepper. In a small bowl, toss cheeses and chiles together. Fold yolks and half of cheese mixture into egg whites.

Heat the butter and oil in a medium nonstick frying pan with ovenproof handles, over medium-high heat. When butter begins to bubble, pour egg mixture evenly into pan. Reduce heat to medium and cook until puffy and lightly browned on the bottom, about 2–4 minutes. Sprinkle remaining cheese over top.

Place pan in oven and bake until omelet is done but the center jiggles slightly and cheese is melted, about 2 minutes. Remove from oven. Loosen edges with a spatula and fold in half. Turn out onto a warm plate and serve with Salsa Verde and sour cream. Makes 2 servings.

WAFFLES RANCHEROS

I cup	**milk**
I tablespoon	**apple cider vinegar**
I	**egg**
$^1/_3$ cup	**vegetable oil**
I cup	**cornmeal**
I cup	**flour**
I tablespoon	**baking powder**
I teaspoon	**baking soda**
I teaspoon	**salt**
I teaspoon	**cayenne pepper sauce**
I	**chipotle pepper in adobo,** seeded, minced
I cup	**fresh or frozen corn,** thawed
2 ounces	**sharp cheddar cheese,** grated
$^1/_2$ cup	**minced jalapeno**
2 cups	**black or refried beans,** heated
6	**eggs,** fried sunny side up
$^1/_2$ cup	**grated cheddar cheese**
I recipe	**Lazy Summer Salsa** (page 72) or **Southwest Enchilada Sauce** (page 77)
	avocado and sour cream, for garnish

In a large bowl, stir together the milk, vinegar, egg, and oil until well combined. In a separate bowl, mix together the cornmeal, flour, baking powder, baking soda, and salt. Stir dry mixture into milk mixture until just combined. Stir in pepper sauce, chipotle, corn, cheese, and jalapeno.

Heat a waffle iron to hottest setting and spray lightly with nonstick cooking spray. Ladle about $^1/_2$ cup batter onto waffle iron and cook until brown and crisp. Repeat with remaining batter. Top waffles with beans, fried eggs, cheese, and salsa or enchilada sauce. Garnish with avocado and sour cream. Makes 6 servings.

CLASSIC CHILAQUILES

4	**Roma tomatoes**
2	**jalapenos,** seeded
I	**medium onion,** peeled
2 tablespoons	**vegetable oil**
4 cloves	**garlic**
I can (4 ounces)	**whole roasted green chiles,** drained, diced
$\frac{1}{2}$ cup	**vegetable stock**
	salt and pepper, to taste
I bag (14 ounces)	**plain tortilla chips**
$\frac{1}{2}$ cup	**Cotija cheese or queso fresco**
I	**large ripe avocado,** diced
	sour cream or Mexican crema
6	**eggs,** poached or sunny side up

Preheat oven to broil.

Cut tomatoes, jalapenos, and onion in half; toss in a bowl with oil to coat. Place on a baking sheet and roast under the broiler until skins are charred, about 15 minutes. Turn vegetables and add garlic to pan halfway through. Remove skins and place in a food processor, chopping into a chunky salsa. Pour salsa, green chiles, and stock into a large frying pan. Bring to a simmer and season with salt and pepper.

Break chips into simmering salsa and stir until well coated, but not soggy. Spoon into a serving dish, sprinkle with cheese, and garnish with avocado and sour cream. Top with eggs, and season with salt and pepper. Makes 6 servings.

CHORIZO AND PAPAS EGG MUFFINS

8 ounces	**soft cooking chorizo**
I cup	**frozen shredded hash browns,** thawed
15	**eggs**
1/3 cup	**grated mild cheddar cheese**
1	**poblano chile,** roasted, seeded, diced
3	**green onions,** thinly sliced
1/2 teaspoon	**salt**
1/4 teaspoon	**pepper**

Preheat oven to 375 degrees. Prepare a 12-cup muffin pan with nonstick cooking spray.

Remove skin from chorizo and brown in frying pan. Remove chorizo from pan with a slotted spoon and drain on paper towels. Cook hash browns in same pan until golden brown.

Beat the eggs in a large bowl and stir in chorizo, hash browns, cheese, chile, onions, salt, and pepper until well combined. Spoon mixture into muffin cups and bake for 20–30 minutes, or until eggs have set and are slightly browned. Makes 12 muffins.

APPETIZERS

BACON-WRAPPED SHRIMP KABOBS

2	**jalapenos,** seeded
2 ounces	**Monterey Jack cheese**
1 package (12 ounces)	**bacon**
24	**medium shrimp,** peeled, deveined
1/2	**fresh pineapple,** peeled, cut into 1-inch cubes
24 (10–12 inch)	**bamboo skewers,** soaked in water
	salsa, optional

Cut jalapenos and cheese into 1/8-inch wide matchstick-size strips. Measure length of bacon needed to wrap around shrimp by wrapping a slice around a shrimp and cutting off excess. Use this piece of bacon as a pattern to cut other slices. Cut a slit down the back of each shrimp a little deeper than you need to devein shrimp. Insert 1 strip of jalapeno and 1 strip of cheese into shrimp. Wrap 1 piece of bacon firmly around each shrimp and secure with a toothpick. Refrigerate until ready to grill.

Thread 1 cube of pineapple onto each skewer followed by 1 shrimp, starting at the tail and running though the top, making sure to skewer the bacon as well. Skewering through the bacon will keep it from curling away from the shrimp when it hits the flames. Grill kabobs on charcoal or gas grill over medium-high heat until bacon is crispy, about 4 minutes on each side. Remove toothpicks before serving. Serve with your favorite salsa. Makes 4–6 servings.

PINEAPPLE-JALAPENO WONTONS

8 ounces	**cream cheese,** at room temperature
I can (8 ounces)	**crushed pineapple,** drained
2	**green onions,** minced
I	**jalapeno,** seeded, minced
24	**wonton wrappers**
	vegetable oil, for frying or baking
⅔ cup	**Avocado-Tomatillo Salsa** (page 74)
½ cup	**drained crushed pineapple**

In a medium bowl, mix together cream cheese, I can of pineapple, onions, and jalapeno. Place I teaspoon of cream cheese mixture into center of a wonton wrapper. Brush edges of wrapper with water. Fold wonton in half diagonally to make a triangle and press to seal edges. Repeat with remaining wontons.

If frying, heat several inches of oil in a large pot to 365 degrees. Fry wontons until golden brown and crispy.

If baking, preheat oven to 350 degrees. Brush wontons with oil, place on a baking sheet that has been prepared with nonstick cooking spray, and bake for 12–15 minutes, or until edges are golden brown and crispy. Drain on paper towels.

For dipping sauce, pulse salsa and ½ cup pineapple together in a food processor until blended. Makes 24 wontons.

CHIPOTLE CHICKEN SPRING ROLLS

4	**boneless, skinless chicken breasts**
2 tablespoons	**vegetable oil,** divided
1 tablespoon	**minced chipotle pepper in adobo**
3 tablespoons	**taco seasoning mix**
12	**rice paper wrappers**
1/2	**English cucumber,** thinly sliced
1 1/2 cups	**cooked rice noodles**
2	**ripe avocados,** thinly sliced
2	**carrots,** peeled, cut into matchsticks
2	**jalapenos,** seeded, minced
2 cups	**baby spinach**
1 teaspoon	**salt**
1/2 teaspoon	**pepper**
1 recipe	**Avocado-Tomatillo Salsa** (page 74)

Rinse chicken and pat dry. In a small bowl, mix together 1 tablespoon oil, chipotle, and seasoning mix to make a paste. Spread chipotle paste on both sides of chicken, cover, and set aside for 30 minutes at room temperature. Preheat grill or grill pan to medium-high heat. Brush grill with remaining 1 tablespoon oil and cook chicken until done, about 4 minutes on each side. Slice cooked chicken into thin strips.

Dip 1 rice paper wrapper into a shallow dish of cold water until softened, about 3–5 seconds. Place wrapper on a plate or cutting board and line cucumber slices across 1/3 of wrapper. Layer chicken, noodles, avocado, carrots, jalapenos, and spinach on top; season with salt and pepper and roll into a burrito shape. Repeat with remaining wrappers. Serve with Avocado Tomatillo Salsa. Makes 12 rolls.

SONORAN-STYLE CHEESE CRISPS

3	**Anaheim chiles,** roasted
	vegetable oil, for frying
4 (10-inch)	**flour tortillas**
2 cups	**grated longhorn or mild cheddar cheese**
	pico de gallo or favorite salsa

Preheat oven to 400 degrees.

Remove stem and seeds from chiles, and dice or cut into thin strips.

Pour enough oil into a 12-inch frying pan to measure ⅓ of the way up the sides of the pan. Heat oil on medium-high until bubbles appear when a small piece of tortilla is placed in the pan. Reduce heat to medium. Fry 1 tortilla at a time until golden brown on each side. Remove and drain on paper towels. Sprinkle evenly with cheese and chiles. Place tortillas on a baking sheet and bake until cheese is melted and bubbly, about 3 minutes. Serve with pico de gallo or favorite salsa. Makes 4 servings.

SHRIMP QUESADILLAS

2 tablespoons	**vegetable oil**
¼ cup	**minced onion**
24	**medium shrimp,** peeled, deveined
I clove	**garlic,** peeled, minced
¼ cup	**white wine or chicken stock**
2	**poblano or Anaheim chiles,** roasted, seeded, thinly sliced
	salt and pepper, to taste
8 ounces	**Oaxaca or Monterey Jack cheese,** grated
4 ounces	**creamy goat cheese,** crumbled
6 (12-inch)	**flour tortillas**
I	**ripe avocado,** diced
	sour cream
	salsa, of choice

Heat oil in a large frying pan over medium-high heat. Saute onion and shrimp until shrimp begin to turn pink, about 2 minutes. Add garlic and saute for I minute. Add wine or stock and reduce until liquid is almost gone. Stir in chiles and heat through. Season with salt and pepper. In a small bowl, mix the two cheeses together.

Place I tortilla on a preheated griddle or large frying pan. Sprinkle some of the cheese over the entire tortilla and some of the shrimp mixture over half of the tortilla. When the cheese melts place some of the avocado on top of the shrimp and fold the tortilla in half. Heat until lightly browned on the bottom then turn quesadilla over to brown other side. Repeat process for each tortilla. Serve with sour cream and salsa. Makes 6 servings.

JALAPENOS IN A BLANKET

I can (8 count)	**crescent roll dough**
4	**jalapenos,** roasted, peeled, seeded, halved
4 ounces	**cream cheese**
4 strips	**bacon,** cooked, chopped
I tablespoon	**Tabasco sauce**

Preheat oven to 375 degrees.

Unroll the dough and separate into 8 triangles. Place I jalapeno half on the wide end of each piece of dough. Cut the cream cheese into 8 sticks and place I on each jalapeno half. Divide bacon pieces between each jalapeno half and top with a few drops of Tabasco sauce.

Roll jalapenos in dough starting at the wide end. Place on a baking sheet, and bake until golden brown, about 12–15 minutes.
Makes 8 appetizers.

CHEESY ENCHILADA MONKEY BREAD

I cup	**butter,** melted
I	**chipotle pepper in adobo,** seeded, minced
2 cloves	**garlic,** peeled, minced
I ½ teaspoons	**red chile powder**
½ teaspoon	**cumin**
½ teaspoon	**salt**
¼ teaspoon	**pepper**
2 cans (16 ounces each)	**buttermilk biscuits,** quartered
2 cups	**grated sharp cheddar cheese**
8 ounces	**cream cheese,** crumbled
2	**green onions,** minced
I	**jalapeno,** roasted, seeded, minced
I cup	**Southwest Enchilada Sauce** (page 77), divided

Preheat oven to 350 degrees. Prepare a 9 x 5-inch loaf pan with nonstick cooking spray.

In a medium bowl, mix together the butter, chipotle, garlic, chile powder, cumin, salt, and pepper. Dip biscuit pieces into the butter mixture and place half in the bottom of prepared pan.

In a separate bowl, toss cheeses, onions, and jalapeno together and layer half the cheese mixture over top of biscuit dough; drizzle with ½ cup enchilada sauce. Make a second layer with remaining biscuit dough and drizzle with remaining ½ cup enchilada sauce; top with remaining cheese mixture. Bake for 20–30 minutes, or until golden brown. Cool for 20 minutes then turn out onto a serving plate. Makes 6–12 servings.

RED CHILE HOME FRIES

2 ½ pounds	**russet potatoes,** peeled
4 tablespoons	**vegetable oil**
1 tablespoon	**salt**
1 teaspoon	**pepper**
4 tablespoons	**Garlic-Chile Oil** (page 121)
¼ cup	**finely grated Parmesan cheese**
¼ cup	**finely grated Gruyere cheese**
1	**Fresno chile or red jalapeno,** seeded, finely minced
1 tablespoon	**minced fresh cilantro**

Preheat oven to 425 degrees.

Wash potatoes well and pat dry. Cut potatoes in half lengthwise. Cut each half into 3 equally sized wedges. Place potatoes in a large bowl and toss with vegetable oil, salt, and pepper. Spread potatoes on a baking sheet and roast for 15 minutes. Remove from oven, turn the potato wedges, and roast until brown and tender, about 10–15 more minutes. Drizzle Garlic-Chile Oil over fries and toss.

In a small bowl, mix Parmesan, Gruyere, minced chile, and cilantro together. Divide fries onto 6 serving plates and garnish with cheese mixture. Makes 6 servings.

ESQUITES (MEXICAN CORN DIP)

6 ears	**sweet corn,** in husk
1	**jalapeno,** seeded, minced
1 teaspoon	**sugar**
¾ cup	**mayonnaise**
1	**lime,** juiced
1 tablespoon	**hot sauce,** such as Tabasco or Cholula
2–3 tablespoons	**vegetable stock**
	salt and freshly ground pepper, to taste
1 teaspoon	**New Mexico red chile powder**
2 ounces	**Cotija or queso fresco cheese,** crumbled (may substitute feta)
1 tablespoon	**minced fresh cilantro**
	corn tortilla chips, warmed
	lime wedges

Roast corn in husks on a grill at medium-high heat until husks are charred and corn is warmed through, about 5 minutes. Or, roast corn in a preheated 450 degree oven for 10–15 minutes, until warmed through. Do not overcook corn. Turn when necessary. When corn is cool enough to handle, remove husks and silks. Cut kernels from the cobs and place in a medium bowl; toss with jalapeno and sugar.

In a large frying pan, mix together the mayonnaise, lime juice, and hot sauce over medium heat. Add vegetable stock, and bring to a simmer; immediately lower heat. Toss corn kernels into sauce and season with salt and pepper.

Pour corn kernels into a bowl or individual serving cups. Sprinkle with chile powder, cheese, and cilantro. Serve with tortilla chips and lime wedges. Makes 6–10 servings.

JALAPENO-CHEDDAR BISCUITS

6 tablespoons	**cold butter,** divided
2 cups	**biscuit mix**
1/2 cup	**cold milk**
1/2 cup	**grated sharp cheddar cheese**
2 tablespoons	**minced jalapeno**
3/4 teaspoon	**garlic powder,** divided
2 tablespoons	**butter**
1/4 teaspoon	**dried cilantro**
1/2 teaspoon	**chile powder**
1/4 teaspoon	**salt**

Preheat oven to 425 degrees.

Cut 4 tablespoons of butter into 1/2-inch cubes and mix together in a large bowl with the biscuit mix, using a fork or pastry cutter until mixture resembles coarse crumbs. Add milk, cheese, jalapeno, and 1/4 teaspoon garlic powder; mix together to form a dough. Do not overmix.

Using a large spoon, drop 1/4-cup sized portions of biscuit mixture onto an ungreased baking sheet. Bake until golden brown, about 10–12 minutes.

Melt remaining 2 tablespoons butter with remaining 1/2 teaspoon garlic powder, cilantro, and chile powder. Brush over biscuits and sprinkle with salt. Makes 4–6 servings.

TEXAS TOTS

10	**dried guajillo chiles,** seeded
10	**dried ancho chiles,** seeded
	boiling water
8 cups	**frozen tater tots**
1 ½	**pounds ground beef**
1	**small yellow onion,** diced
5 cloves	**garlic,** minced
	salt, to taste
1 ½ teaspoons	**dried Mexican oregano leaves,** crushed
1 teaspoon	**cumin**
2 cups	**finely grated cheddar cheese**
¼ cup	**sliced green onions**
	sour cream
4–6	**eggs,** cooked sunny side up, or to liking, optional

Preheat oven to 425 degrees.

Place chiles in a large bowl and cover with boiling water; soak for 10 minutes. Place rehydrated chiles in a blender with ¼ cup of the soaking water and puree; set aside.

Prepare tater tots according to package directions.

In a large frying pan over medium heat, brown the ground beef, onion, and garlic until meat is no longer pink; drain grease. Return pan to heat and add the chile puree, salt, oregano, and cumin. Bring to a simmer and cook until thickened, about 20–30 minutes, stirring occasionally. Spoon red chile beef over tater tots and garnish with cheese, green onions, sour cream, and eggs. Makes 6 servings.

CHILE-CHEESE GARLIC BREAD

½ cup	**unsalted butter**
I teaspoon	**red chile powder**
3 cloves	**garlic,** peeled, mashed into a paste
I loaf (12 inches)	**French bread**
¼ teaspoon	**salt**
2	**Anaheim chiles or jalapenos,** roasted, peeled, seeded
2 cups	**grated white cheddar cheese**
2 cups	**grated Monterey Jack cheese**
¼ cup	**freshly grated Parmesan cheese**

Preheat oven to 375 degrees.

In a small saucepan, melt the butter with the chile powder and garlic. Cut bread lengthwise into 2 long halves and place on a baking sheet. Brush butter mixture generously over cut sides of bread, sprinkle with salt, and toast in oven until lightly brown, about 4 minutes.

Remove bread from oven. Finely dice the chiles and sprinkle evenly over bread. In a medium bowl, mix the cheeses together and sprinkle over bread. Return bread to oven and toast until cheese is melted, bubbly, and beginning to brown around the edges, about 6–8 minutes. Cut into slices. Makes 6 servings.

MUSHROOM-POBLANO QUESO FUNDIDO

2 tablespoons	**butter**
1/3 cup	**thinly sliced cremini mushrooms**
1 teaspoon	**minced garlic**
1 tablespoon	**flour**
3/4 cup	**milk**
1/2 teaspoon	**salt**
1/4 teaspoon	**pepper**
1	**large poblano chile,** roasted, seeded, sliced into 1/4-inch strips
12 ounces	**Monterey Jack cheese,** grated
4 ounces	**creamy goat cheese**
	pico de gallo, minced fresh cilantro, salsa, and sour cream, for garnish

Preheat oven to broil.

In a medium frying pan over medium-high heat, melt the butter and saute mushrooms for about 2–3 minutes. Add garlic and flour, and cook, stirring for 2 minutes more. Pour in milk, stirring to combine and bring to a boil. Add salt, pepper, and chile strips; remove from heat. Stir in Monterey Jack cheese until melted.

Pour queso into a buttered, ovenproof serving dish, crumble goat cheese over the top, and heat under broiler until goat cheese is golden brown. Garnish with pico de gallo, cilantro, salsa, and sour cream as desired. Serve with warm tortillas or corn chips. Makes 6 servings.

JALAPENO CORN FRITTERS WITH BACON

3	**eggs,** separated
1 can (15 ounces)	**corn,** with liquid
¾ cup	**flour**
1 teaspoon	**baking soda**
1 teaspoon	**salt**
1	**jalapeno,** seeded, finely minced
	vegetable oil
	Chipotle Mayonnaise (page 120)
3	**green onions,** thinly sliced
6 strips	**bacon,** cooked, crumbled

In a medium bowl, whip egg whites to medium peaks; set aside.

In a large bowl, beat egg yolks until pale yellow. Add the corn, flour, baking soda, salt, and jalapeno. Stir until flour is well blended. Fold ⅓ of the egg whites into corn mixture to lighten up the batter, which should be the consistency of thick pancake batter. Gently fold remaining egg whites into batter. Cover and refrigerate for 15–20 minutes.

Pour 2 inches of oil into the bottom of a large, deep saucepan (no more than ⅓ of the way full) and heat to 360 degrees.

Remove batter from refrigerator and stir to evenly distribute corn and jalapeno. Spray a spoon with nonstick baking spray so that batter will slip off spoon easier. Drop tablespoon-sized spoonfuls of batter into oil and fry until golden brown, about 2–4 minutes. Turn fritters halfway through. Remove fritters from oil and drain on a paper towel. To serve, drizzle with Chipotle Mayonnaise and garnish with green onions and bacon. Makes about 2 dozen bite-size fritters.

SAVORY CHIPOTLE CHILE CHEESECAKE

1 ½ cups	**stoneground cracker crumbs**
3 tablespoons	**unsalted butter,** melted
16 ounces	**cream cheese,** softened
2 tablespoons	**sugar**
1	**egg**
¼ cup	**diced onion**
2 cloves	**garlic,** peeled, minced
2	**chipotle peppers in adobo,** seeded, minced
1	**medium tomato,** seeded, finely diced **crackers or sliced vegetables**

Preheat oven to 325 degrees. Prepare a 6-inch springform pan with nonstick cooking spray.

In a small bowl, mix cracker crumbs and butter together and press evenly into bottom of prepared pan. Bake until lightly toasted and fragrant, about 3–4 minutes.

In a medium bowl, beat cream cheese and sugar together for 2–3 minutes. Beat in egg. Mix onion, garlic, chipotles, and tomato into cheese mixture. Pour batter over crust and smooth out evenly. Bake until cheesecake is puffy and begins to pull away from sides, about 45–55 minutes. The center should still be jiggly. Remove from oven and cool for 2 hours. Cover and refrigerate for 1–2 hours before serving. Serve with crackers or sliced vegetables. Makes 10–12 servings.

SOUPS, SALADS, AND SANDWICHES

JICAMA-ORANGE SALAD WITH CHILE-LIME VINAIGRETTE

2	**medium Valencia oranges**
I	**medium jicama,** peeled, diced
I	**tomato,** seeded, diced
1/4	**red onion,** very thinly sliced
2 tablespoons	**minced fresh cilantro**
2	**limes,** zested
1/4 cup	**fresh lime juice**
2 tablespoons	**red chile powder**
1/2 cup	**honey**
2 tablespoons	**light olive oil**
I	**habanero, Fresno, or jalapeno chile,** seeded
	salt and pepper, to taste

Cut oranges into supremes (cut peel away from orange and cut orange segments away from interior membrane), dice orange segments into 1/2-inch cubes. Toss in a medium bowl with jicama, tomato, onion, and cilantro.

Place the lime zest, juice, chile powder, honey, olive oil, and chile in a blender; blend until smooth. Pour over salad and season with salt and pepper. Makes 4–6 servings.

ENSALADA DE NOCHE BUENA (CHRISTMAS EVE SALAD)

6 cups	**mixed salad greens**
1	**jalapeno,** seeded, finely diced
1	**red Fresno chile,** seeded, finely diced
1	**small jicama,** peeled, cut into matchsticks
3	**tangerines,** peeled, sliced into rounds
2	**ripe avocados,** diced
1/3 cup	**pepitas,** toasted
1/2 cup	**pomegranate seeds**
4 ounces	**creamy goat cheese,** crumbled
1/2 teaspoon	**red chile flakes,** optional
1 recipe	**Jalapeno-Orange Vinaigrette** (page 174)

Divide greens onto 6 plates. In a small bowl, mix together the jalapeno and chile and sprinkle evenly over the greens. Divide the jicama, tangerines, avocados, pepitas, pomegranate seeds, and cheese between the salad plates. Sprinkle with chile flakes and drizzle with Jalapeno-Orange Vinaigrette. Makes 6 servings.

Variation: If you prefer to serve family style, place all ingredients in a large bowl and toss with 1/3 cup of vinaigrette, or more if desired.

TOPOPO SALAD

2 packages (1 ounce each)	**taco seasoning mix**
4–6	**boneless, skinless chicken breasts**
1 cup	**orange juice**
2 tablespoons	**lime juice**
¼ cup	**olive oil**
½	**red onion,** thinly sliced
2 cloves	**garlic,** peeled, minced
1	**habanero chile,** seeded, minced
	salt and pepper, to taste
4–6 cups	**mixed greens**
1 recipe	**Chile-Lime Vinaigrette** (page 113)
2	**Hatch red chiles,** roasted, seeded, cut into strips
2	**Anaheim or poblano chiles,** roasted, seeded, cut into strips
1	**large mango,** peeled, cut into strips
1	**jicama or cucumber,** peeled, cut into strips

Sprinkle taco seasoning evenly over chicken on both sides. Place chicken in a glass or plastic dish. In a small bowl, combine juices, oil, onion, garlic, and habanero. Stir to combine; pour over chicken. Cover and marinate in refrigerator for 2–4 hours. Remove chicken from the marinade and season with salt and pepper on both sides. Discard marinade. Cook chicken on a grill or grill pan over medium-high heat until cooked all the way through, about 6–8 minutes on each side. Remove from heat and cut into strips.

Toss greens with vinaigrette and divide into 6 even portions, making a pile in the center of each plate. Arrange strips of chicken, chiles, mango, and jicama or cucumber vertically around the greens to resemble a volcano with streams of lava flowing down. Makes 6 servings.

GREEN CHILE CAPRESE SALAD

4	**medium tomatoes** (stem on, if possible)
2 balls (8 ounces each)	**fresh mozzarella**
3	**Anaheim or Hatch chiles,** roasted, seeded, diced
	salt, to taste
	freshly ground pepper, to taste
½ cup	**Green Chile Pesto** (page 118)
4 tablespoons	**balsamic vinegar**
1 cup	**chopped baby arugula leaves**

Rinse and dry tomatoes. Cut the tomatoes crosswise into slices slightly under ½-inch thick but more than ¼-inch thick, so they will hold up well when stacked. Slice a small piece off the bottom of each tomato so they will stand firm. Slice mozzarella in the same manner as tomatoes.

Assemble salads by placing the bottom of a tomato on a serving plate. Place a spoonful of diced chiles on each slice of tomato. Season with salt and pepper. Place a slice of mozzarella on tomato and drizzle with pesto and a few drops of balsamic vinegar. Top with arugula. Repeat layers until tomato has been reconstructed.

Garnish with drizzles of pesto, dots of balsamic vinegar, and a few arugula leaves. Serve at room temperature for the cheese to have maximum flavor. Makes 4 servings.

MANGO CRAB SALAD

¹/₂ pound	**chilled fresh cooked crabmeat or cocktail-sized shrimp**
2 tablespoons	**cold mayonnaise**
I tablespoon	**minced green onion**
¹/₂	**ripe mango,** finely diced
¹/₂	**red bell pepper,** seeded, finely diced
I	**jalapeno,** seeded, minced
	salt and pepper, to taste
2	**large ripe avocados**
I tablespoon	**lime juice**
	fresh cilantro, for garnish, optional

In a medium bowl, mix crab with mayonnaise and green onion. Gently fold mango, bell pepper, and jalapeno into crab mixture. Season with salt and pepper.

Cut avocados in half lengthwise and remove pits. Brush surface of avocados with lime juice to prevent discoloration. Cut a small slice off bottoms of each avocado half so they will sit level on a plate. Place avocado halves on serving plates and generously heap crab salad into each half. Garnish with cilantro. Makes 4 servings.

OLD WORLD POSOLE

2 pounds	**boneless pork shoulder**
½ cup	**regular Coca-Cola**
½ cup	**fresh orange juice**
2 teaspoons	**cumin**
3 tablespoons	**chile powder**
1	**medium yellow onion,** chopped
2	**poblano or Anaheim chiles,** seeded, minced
2	**carrots,** peeled, sliced
3 cloves	**garlic,** peeled, minced
2 cups	**vegetable or chicken stock**
2 cans (15 ounces each)	**hominy,** drained
¼ cup	**chopped fresh cilantro**
¼ cup	**radish matchsticks,** optional
4–6 (10-inch)	**flour tortillas**

Cut pork shoulder into 4 equal pieces and place in a slow cooker. In a small bowl, mix together the Coca-Cola, orange juice, cumin, and chile powder and pour over the pork. Add the onion, chiles, carrots, and garlic. Pour in stock and cover. Cook on low until pork is tender and can be pulled apart with a fork, about 6–8 hours.

Add hominy during the last 2 hours of cooking. Remove pork from slow cooker and allow to cool enough to handle; shred. Return shredded pork to slow cooker. Garnish individual servings with cilantro and radishes. Serve with warm tortillas. Makes 6–8 servings.

MEXICAN MEATBALL SOUP

2 tablespoons	**vegetable oil**
1	**small yellow onion,** diced
1	**carrot,** peeled, sliced
1 cup	**peeled and diced potato**
1	**poblano or Anaheim chile,** seeded, diced
2 teaspoons	**dried Mexican oregano leaves,** crushed
1/2 teaspoon	**cumin**
1	**zucchini,** seeded, diced
1 can (15 ounces)	**diced tomatoes,** drained
4 cups	**chicken or vegetable stock**
1 cup	**water**
1 1/2	**teaspoons salt**
1/2 teaspoon	**pepper**
1 recipe	**Mexican Meatballs** (page 60)
1 cup	**corn kernels**
3 cups	**cooked rice,** optional

Heat oil in a large pot over medium heat. Add onion, carrot, potato, and chile. Cook until onion is translucent and potato is tender, about 5 minutes. Stir in oregano, cumin, and zucchini; cook for 2 minutes. Add tomatoes, stock, water, salt, and pepper. Bring to a boil then reduce heat and simmer for 15 minutes. Add meatballs and corn and simmer until meatballs are cooked through and hot. Divide rice, if desired, between 6 serving bowls and ladle soup over top. Makes 6 servings.

GRILLED CHEESE DEL MAR

20–24	**medium shrimp,** peeled, deveined
1 packet (1 ounce)	**taco seasoning mix**
2 tablespoons	**vegetable oil**
2 tablespoons	**minced shallot**
2 cloves	**garlic,** peeled, minced
1 can (12 ounces)	**diced green chiles, or 3 jalapenos,** roasted, seeded, diced
8 slices	**soft French bread,** ¾-inch thick
½ cup	**butter,** melted
2 cups	**finely grated Monterey Jack cheese**
4 ounces	**sour cream**
2 tablespoons	**diced pickled jalapenos**
	salt and pepper, to taste

Place shrimp in a medium bowl and add taco seasoning; toss to coat. Heat oil in a large frying pan over medium heat. Add shallot, garlic, and shrimp. Saute shrimp for 3–4 minutes on each side, or until pink and opaque. Remove cooked shrimp from pan and drain on paper towels. Add green chiles to pan and heat through. Remove from heat.

Brush 1 side of each slice of bread with melted butter. Place 2 slices of bread buttered side down in a separate frying pan. Layer ¼ of the grated cheese, green chiles, sour cream, and cooked shrimp on each slice of bread. Sprinkle with jalapenos and season with salt and pepper. Top with a second slice of bread, buttered side up. Grill sandwiches slowly over medium heat until golden brown and crispy on the bottom; flip and grill other side. Cook until sandwiches are toasted and cheese has melted. Repeat. Makes 4 servings.

SONORAN BACON-
WRAPPED HOT DOGS

10 strips	**bacon**
1 package (10 count)	**hot dogs**
1 can (15 ounces)	**ranch-style beans,** drained and heated
10	**Mexican bolillos or other soft, crusty rolls**
2	**ripe avocados,** diced
1 cup	**Lazy Summer Salsa** (page 72) **or pico de gallo**
1/2 bunch	**cilantro,** minced
10	**mild chiles such as guero or Amarillo,** roasted, sliced
1 cup	**Chipotle Mayonnaise** (page 120)

Wrap 1 strip of bacon around each hot dog and secure with a toothpick. Grill bacon-wrapped hot dogs over medium heat until bacon is crispy on all sides. Cook slowly and turn hot dogs often so that hot dogs are heated through by the time bacon crisps, about 10 minutes.

To serve, place a spoonful of beans on the bottom of each roll. Add a hot dog, some avocado, and salsa or pico de gallo. Top with cilantro and chiles, and drizzle with Chipotle Mayonnaise. Makes 10 servings.

GREEN CHILE GRILLED CHEESE SANDWICH

6 ounces	**Parmesan cheese,** grated
1/2 cup	**butter,** softened
12 slices	**sourdough bread**
6 slices	**Muenster cheese**
6 slices	**Swiss cheese**
6 slices	**cheddar cheese**
2	**poblano chiles,** roasted, peeled, seeded, cut into strips
6 strips	**bacon,** cooked, crumbled

Sprinkle Parmesan cheese on a plate. Butter 1 side of each slice of bread and place buttered side in Parmesan cheese. Place bread slices on a baking sheet, cheese side up.

Heat a large frying pan or griddle over medium heat, and place 1 slice of bread cheese side down in pan. Layer 1 slice of each type of cheese on bread and top with jalapeno strips and crumbled bacon. Top with a second piece of bread, cheese side up, and cook until golden brown on the bottom; flip and grill other side until golden brown. Repeat. Makes 6 servings.

ROASTED VEGETABLE SANDWICH

2	**Japanese eggplants**
2	**zucchini**
	vegetable oil
2	**red bell peppers**
2	**poblano chiles**
	salt and pepper, to taste
4	**ciabatta rolls**
I recipe	**Chipotle Mayonnaise** (page 120)
8 ounces	**queso panela or fresh mozzarella cheese**
I tablespoon	**dried Mexican oregano leaves**
I bunch	**fresh spinach**

Slice eggplants and zucchini lengthwise into long 1/4-inch-thick slices. Very lightly, oil eggplant and zucchini slices, bell peppers, and poblanos, and place on a grill (a grill pan works great and isn't as messy) over medium-high heat. Cook until grill marks form, but vegetables are still firm and al dente. Season with salt and pepper. Sprinkle vegetables generously with salt after they are taken off the grill so they do not let off too much of their juices. Dice eggplant slices. Remove peels and seeds from peppers and poblanos; cut into strips.

Cut rolls in half, brush lightly with oil, and toast lightly on grill. Spread Chipotle Mayonnaise on rolls and layer on the vegetables. Warm cheese quickly on grill, slice, and add to sandwiches. Season with oregano, salt, and pepper, and top with spinach. Makes 4 servings.

GREEN CHILE MEATBALL SUBS

1	**red onion,** thinly sliced
1 cup	**boiling water**
1/2 cup	**orange juice**
1/2 cup	**lime juice**
1/2 teaspoon	**salt,** plus extra
1 recipe	**Mexican Meatballs** (page 60)
2 1/2 cups	**Salsa Verde** (page 75)
6	**Mexican bolillos or soft hoagie rolls**
1 1/2 cups	**grated Monterey Jack cheese**
	onion slices, for garnish
3	**jalapenos,** fresh or bottled, thinly sliced
	sour cream, optional

Put onion in a glass or plastic bowl and cover with boiling water. Let sit for 30 seconds then drain. Pour juices over onion and stir in 1/2 teaspoon salt. Set aside.

Place meatballs in a large frying pan with the Salsa Verde and sprinkle with salt, to taste. Bring to a boil, reduce heat to low, and simmer until meatballs are cooked and heated through, about 20–30 minutes.

Preheat oven to 400 degrees.

Slice the bolillos lengthwise, but not all the way through. Spoon meatballs and some sauce into rolls. Top with cheese and place on a baking sheet. Heat in oven until cheese is melted and rolls are warm. Drain onions. Garnish sandwiches with onion slices, jalapenos, and sour cream. Makes 6 servings.

GRILLED STRAWBERRY SALSA SANDWICH

2 tablespoons	**Garlic-Chile Oil** (page 121)
3 tablespoons	**finely diced onion**
1	**Fresno chile or jalapeno,** seeded, minced
1 quart	**strawberries,** sliced
1/2 bunch	**fresh cilantro,** chopped
1	**lime,** juiced
	salt and pepper, to taste
4 tablespoons	**butter,** softened
12 thin slices	**sourdough or French bread**
10 ounces	**Saint Andre or Brie cheese**

Heat chile oil in a large frying pan over medium-high heat. Saute onion and chile until soft but not brown. Remove from pan and drain on paper towels. Place strawberries in a medium bowl and add the onion and chile mixture. When cool, add cilantro and lime juice. Season with salt and pepper.

Butter 1 side of each slice of bread and place on a cutting board butter side down. Remove rind from cheese and slice thinly. Lay 1 slice of cheese on 6 slices of bread, and top with a scoop of strawberry salsa; cover with another slice of cheese. Place remaining slices of bread buttered side up on each sandwich.

Heat a nonstick griddle or frying pan on medium-high heat. Place a sandwich in the pan, reduce heat to medium, and cook until golden brown on the bottom and cheese is melted; flip and grill other side until golden brown. Repeat. Makes 6 servings.

MAIN DISHES

CARNE ASADA STREET TACOS

2 pounds	**beef fillet or sirloin steak**
I recipe	**Carne Asada Marinade** (page 122)
	salt and pepper, to taste
2 tablespoons	**vegetable oil**
24 (4-inch)	**corn tortillas,** warmed
	guacamole
	salsa or pico de gallo
I cup	**grated Monterey Jack**
	or Cotija cheese
¼ cup	**sour cream**
2	**jalapenos or Fresno chiles,**
	seeded, thinly sliced

Cut beef into long strips, I inch wide by I inch thick. Place beef strips and marinade in a large ziplock bag and marinate in refrigerator for 4–6 hours. Remove beef from bag and discard excess marinade. Season beef with salt and pepper.

Heat oil in a large frying pan on medium-high and sear the beef strips for 2–3 minutes on each side. Beef should be medium rare in center. Remove from heat and let rest for about 15 minutes. Slice strips into ¼-inch-thick slices.

Assemble tacos by stacking 2 tortillas together. Spread guacamole on top of each tortilla and layer on sliced beef, salsa, and cheese. Top with sour cream and chiles. Makes 12 tacos.

SOUR CREAM ENCHILADAS

	vegetable oil, for frying
18 (6-inch)	**corn tortillas**
4 ounces	**unsalted butter**
¼ cup	**flour**
1 can (6 ounces)	**diced green chiles**
2 cups	**chicken or vegetable stock**
8 ounces	**sour cream**
	salt, to taste
16 ounces	**Monterey Jack cheese,** grated
1	**small white onion,** finely diced

Preheat oven to 350 degrees.

Heat ½ inch oil in a frying pan over medium heat. Soften tortillas by dipping them in the warmed oil for a few seconds on each side. For faster results, dip 2 at a time. This will also prevent tortillas from getting crisp too quickly. Drain on paper towels.

Melt butter in a large saucepan over medium-high heat. When butter begins to foam, add flour. Stir and cook until flour is absorbed, but not browned. Add chiles and stock, stirring to combine. Bring to a boil. Reduce heat and simmer until sauce thickens, stirring constantly. Remove from heat and stir in sour cream. Thin with a little milk if necessary to reach a gravy consistency. Season with salt.

Spread ½ cup of sauce in the bottom of a 9 x 13-inch pan. Place 3–4 tablespoons of cheese and a little onion in the center of each tortilla. Roll enchiladas and place seam side down in the pan on top of sauce. Pour remaining sauce equally over enchiladas and top with remaining cheese and onion. Bake for about 35–45 minutes, or until bubbly. Makes 6–8 servings.

MAYAN-SPICED GRILLED PORK CHOPS

2	**large ripe mangoes,** peeled, diced
1	**large lime,** zested, juiced
1	**habanero chile,** seeded, chopped
2 cloves	**garlic,** peeled, minced
1 tablespoon	**achiote paste**
1 teaspoon	**dried Mexican oregano leaves**
8	**whole allspice berries,** crushed, toasted
1/2 teaspoon	**cumin seeds,** toasted
1 1/4 cups	**water**
1 teaspoon	**freshly ground pepper**
2 tablespoons	**kosher salt**
1/2 cup	**sugar**
2 tablespoons	**white vinegar**
6	**bone-in pork loin chops,** Frenched, trimmed
1 recipe	**Mayan-Spiced Mango Sauce** (page 80)

Place mangoes in a blender with lime zest, juice, chile, garlic, achiote paste, and spices; blend well. Mix in water, pepper, salt, sugar, and vinegar. Pour marinade into a 9-inch glass baking dish and submerge chops in marinade, leaving bones above the surface. Marinate for 4–6 hours in refrigerator, turning occasionally. Remove chops from marinade and bring to room temperature. Cover bones with foil. Place chops on grill preheated to medium heat and spoon marinade over top. Discard remaining marinade. Grill for 5–6 minutes on each side, watching the temperature carefully (internal temperature for medium rare is 145 degrees, and 160 for medium). Allow chops to rest for about 3 minutes. Remove foil from bones. Serve with Mayan-Spiced Mango Sauce. Makes 6 servings.

BAJA SEAFOOD CHILE RELLENO

6	**large poblano chiles,** roasted, peeled
1	**shallot,** minced
1 clove	**garlic,** minced
1	**jalapeno,** seeded, minced
2 tablespoons	**vegetable oil**
1 pound	**medium shrimp,** peeled, deveined
8 ounces	**bay scallops**
1/4 cup	**white wine,** optional
1/2 cup	**heavy cream**
	salt and white pepper, to taste
4 ounces	**Monterey Jack cheese,** grated
2 ounces	**creamy goat cheese,** crumbled
2 cups	**Tomatillo Cream Sauce** (page 78)

Preheat oven to 350 degrees.

Cut a slit lengthwise down roasted chiles, making sure to keep chiles intact for stuffing, and remove seeds.

In a large frying pan, saute shallot, garlic, and jalapeno in oil over medium-high heat until soft but not brown, about 2 minutes. Add shrimp and scallops and saute for about 3 minutes. Add wine and simmer until wine is almost evaporated. Pour in cream and bring to a boil. Season with salt and pepper. Remove from heat and transfer to a bowl.

Divide shrimp mixture into 6 equal portions and stuff into chiles. In a small bowl, mix the cheeses together and stuff a little inside each chile. Place chiles on a baking sheet, top with remaining cheese, and heat in oven until cheese has melted, about 8–10 minutes. Transfer to a serving plate and ladle Tomatillo Cream Sauce over top. Makes 6 servings.

CRISPY SHRIMP TACOS

I	**large ripe avocado,** diced
I	**orange,** zested, juiced
I	**large mango,** peeled, diced
I	**white onion,** diced
I	**jalapeno,** seeded, minced
	salt and pepper, to taste
2 pounds	**frozen battered shrimp,** without tails
½ cup	**Chipotle Mayonnaise** (page 120)
8–12 (4 inch)	**flour tortillas**
	shredded cabbage
	Mexican crema
	Salsa Verde (page 75)

In a small bowl, toss avocado in orange juice and mix in mango, onion, jalapeno, and I teaspoon zest. Season with salt and pepper. Cover with plastic wrap and set aside.

Bake or fry shrimp according to package directions. Working in small batches, spread a few spoonfuls of Chipotle Mayonnaise around the inside of a large bowl. Add hot shrimp, cover bowl with plastic wrap, and toss shrimp to coat. Remove coated shrimp to a separate dish and repeat with remaining shrimp.

To assemble tacos, spoon avocado mixture on tortilla, and top with shrimp, shredded cabbage, crema, and salsa. Makes 4–6 servings.

CHILE RELLENO CON PAPAS

4	**medium russet potatoes**
6 tablespoons	**butter**
1/2 cup	**sour cream**
2 teaspoons	**seasoned salt**
1/2 teaspoon	**pepper**
1/4 cup	**milk**
1/2 cup	**grated cheddar cheese,** divided
2	**large green onions,** finely sliced, divided
4 strips	**bacon,** cooked, crumbed, divided
6	**large poblano chiles,** roasted

Preheat oven to 400 degrees.

Scrub potatoes and pierce in several places with a fork. Bake until fork tender, about 50–60 minutes. Remove from oven and let sit until cool enough to handle. Lower oven temperature to 350 degrees.

Peel and dice potatoes and place in a large mixing bowl. Add the butter, sour cream, salt, and pepper and mix on low speed with a handheld mixer. Add milk a little at a time to make sure potatoes are moist but not soggy. Stir in half the cheddar cheese, green onions, and bacon.

Cut a slit lengthwise down roasted chiles and remove peels and seeds. Fill chiles with potato mixture, and place on a baking sheet; top with the remaining cheese. Bake until potatoes are completely warm and cheese is melted, about 8–10 minutes. Garnish with remaining green onions and bacon. Makes 6 servings.

NAVAJO TACOS

1 pound	**leg of lamb, beef flank, skirt steak, or sirloin steak**
1 recipe	**Carne Asada Marinade** (page 122)
12 pieces	**frozen dinner roll dough**
	oil, for frying, plus 1 tablespoon
	salt and pepper, to taste
6	**Anaheim or Hatch chiles**
1 recipe	**Salsa Verde** (page 75)
	pico de gallo, sour cream, avocado, and Cotija cheese, for garnish

Place meat in glass dish, cover with marinade, and refrigerate for 3–4 hours.

Thaw dough according to package directions. While dough is still cold, combine 2 rolls together and roll into a ball. Repeat process to form 6 balls. Let dough rise until doubled in size. When ready to cook, heat about 2 inches of oil in a large, deep saucepan over medium-high heat to 375 degrees. Stretch dough into thin 6-inch circles. Pinch 2 small holes in dough and fry in hot oil until golden brown, about 15 seconds per side. Drain on paper towels.

Remove meat from marinade, season liberally with salt and pepper, and grill to desired degree of doneness. Cut meat into strips. Lightly coat chiles with 1 tablespoon oil and roast while grilling meat.

Navajo tacos are traditionally served by placing several strips of meat and 1 whole roasted chile on a warm fry bread, folding over like a taco. Serve with Salsa Verde and garnish as desired. Makes 6 servings.

Note: Fry bread is best when taken straight out of fryer. Try to time frying the dough when meat is cooking.

CHICKEN CHILE VERDE

4 tablespoons	**vegetable oil,** divided
2 ½ pounds	**boneless, skinless chicken breasts,** cut into 1-inch cubes
1 cup	**diced yellow onion**
2 teaspoons	**salt**
¾ teaspoon	**pepper**
12	**tomatillos,** husks removed
2	**serrano chiles or jalapenos**
2	**Anaheim chiles**
4 cloves	**garlic**
3 cups	**chicken stock**
8	**bay leaves**
1 cup	**chopped roasted poblano chiles**
½ cup	**chopped fresh cilantro**
	flour tortillas, warmed

Preheat heat oven to 450 degrees.

Heat 2 tablespoons oil in a large Dutch oven over medium-high heat. Add chicken and brown on all sides. Add onion, salt, and pepper. Cook chicken until tender, about 5 minutes.

Place tomatillos, serranos, Anaheim chiles, garlic, and remaining oil in a large bowl and toss to coat. Place on a baking sheet and roast in oven until skins are blistered and charred. Remove skins, stems, and seeds from chiles and chop. Place tomatillos, chopped serrano and Anaheim chiles, and garlic in a blender and puree. Pour chile puree and stock into chicken mixture and add bay leaves. Cook on low heat for 20–30 minutes; remove bay leaves. Stir in chopped poblano and cilantro. Serve with warm flour tortillas. Makes 6 servings.

CHICKEN FLAUTAS

4 tablespoons	**butter**
I	**Anaheim or Hatch chile,** seeded, minced
¼ cup	**minced white onion**
2 tablespoons	**flour**
I teaspoon	**salt**
I cup	**chicken broth**
I tablespoon	**minced fresh cilantro**
I tablespoon	**lime juice**
I teaspoon	**New Mexico red chile powder**
¼ teaspoon	**cumin**
¼ teaspoon	**pepper**
2½ cups	**chopped cooked chicken**
12 (6-inch)	**flour tortillas**
	oil, for frying
	guacamole, grated cheese, **salsa,** for serving

In a large saucepan over medium-high heat, melt butter and saute the chile and onion until tender; stir in flour and salt. Add chicken broth, cook and stir until mixture thickens. Add cilantro, lime juice, chile powder, cumin, and pepper. Stir in chicken, remove from heat, and cool slightly.

Place about 3 tablespoons of chicken mixture down the center of each tortilla. Roll tightly, securing with a wooden toothpick. Heat about 3–4 inches of oil to 300 degrees in a large saucepan or deep fryer. Working in batches, fry flautas for I–2 minutes, or until golden brown. Remove from oil and drain on paper towels. Allow oil to come back up to temperature before starting a new batch. Remove toothpicks before serving. Serve with guacamole, grated cheese, and salsa. Makes 6 servings.

PORTOBELLO MUSHROOM FAJITAS

½ cup	**red wine vinegar**
½ cup	**Worcestershire sauce**
½ cup	**vegetable oil**
¼ cup	**fresh lime juice**
¼ cup	**soy sauce**
½ cup	**cilantro leaves**
3 tablespoons	**minced garlic,** divided
2 tablespoons	**minced jalapeno**
4 large	**portobello mushrooms**
½ cup	**finely sliced white onion**
¼ cup	**finely sliced poblano chile**
	salt and pepper, to taste
1 cup	**crumbled Cotija cheese**
1 recipe	**Chimichurri Salsa** (page 79)
	flour tortillas, warmed

In a large bowl, mix together the vinegar, Worcestershire sauce, oil, lime juice, soy sauce, cilantro, 2 tablespoons garlic, and jalapeno.

Clean mushrooms and remove the stems and gills. Cut mushrooms in half, place in marinade, and allow to sit in refrigerator for 1 hour. (If left for longer than 1 hour, the taste will be too strong).

Remove mushrooms from marinade and slice into thin strips. In a large frying pan over medium-high heat, saute mushrooms, onion, poblano, and remaining tablespoon of garlic for 2 minutes. Carefully pour marinade into pan and cook vegetables until tender, about 6 minutes. Season with salt and pepper. Serve with Cotija cheese, Chimichurri Salsa, and warm tortillas. Makes 4 servings.

MEXICAN MEATBALLS

1 pound	**ground pork**
1	**egg**
3 cloves	**garlic,** peeled, minced
1/2 cup	**minced fresh cilantro**
1/4 cup	**grated Parmesan cheese**
1 tablespoon	**New Mexico red chile powder**
1/2 teaspoon	**cayenne pepper**
1 teaspoon	**cumin**
2 teaspoons	**ground Mexican oregano**
3/4 cup	**panko breadcrumbs or saltine crackers**
1/2 teaspoon	**pepper**
2 tablespoons	**vegetable oil**
2 3/4 cups	**chicken stock**
	enchilada sauce or Salsa Verde, (page 75), for serving
	grated cheese, for serving
	minced fresh cilantro, for serving

In a large bowl, mix together the pork and egg. In a separate bowl, combine garlic, cilantro, Parmesan, chile powder, cayenne, cumin, oregano, breadcrumbs, and pepper. Mix well. Add dry mixture to meat mixture and mix well until evenly combined. Do not overwork the meat. Roll meat into 1-inch meatballs.

Heat oil in a large frying pan on medium-high heat. Cook meatballs until brown on all sides, about 3 minutes. Drain grease from pan. Pour in chicken stock, cover pan, and continue to cook meatballs until no longer pink in the center and stock has reduced, about 5 minutes.

Serve meatballs with enchilada sauce or Salsa Verde, grated cheese, and minced cilantro. They are also perfect for Mexican Meatball Soup (page 42) or in Green Chile Meatball Subs (page 47). Makes 4–6 servings.

SIDE DISHES

CHEESY CALABACITAS

2	**medium zucchini**
2	**yellow squash**
1	**poblano pepper or 1 can (3 ounces) diced green chiles,** drained
1 1/2 tablespoons	**butter**
1	**small yellow onion,** diced
4 ounces	**low-fat cheddar cheese,** grated
	salt and pepper, to taste

Cut zucchini and squash in half lengthwise and remove seeds. Cut into 1/2-inch-thick slices. Remove stem and seeds from poblano and dice.

Melt butter in a large frying pan over medium-high heat and saute onion and fresh chiles until tender, about 5 minutes. Add the zucchini and yellow squash and saute until squash is fork tender but still a little firm. Sprinkle with cheese and stir until melted. Season with salt and pepper. Serve immediately. Makes 6 servings.

MEXICAN STREET CORN ON THE COB

6 ears	**sweet corn,** in husk
I cup	**mayonnaise**
2	**chipotle peppers in adobo,** seeded, minced
1/2 cup	**sour cream**
1/4 cup	**grated Cotija or Parmesan cheese**
1 1/2 tablespoons	**New Mexico red chile powder**
3 tablespoons	**minced fresh cilantro**
2	**limes,** cut into wedges

Cut tips off corn, leaving stem end. Peel husks back and tie together with a husk making a handle to hold the corn. Wash away silks.

Cook corn over a hot grill or in an oven at 400 degrees until slightly charred. Turn corn to cook evenly.

In a small bowl, mix mayonnaise, chipotles, and sour cream together and brush on corn while still warm. Roll the corn in the cheese and sprinkle with chile powder, cilantro, and a spritz of lime. Makes 6 servings.

GREEN CHILE MAC 'N' CHEESE

2 cups	**dry elbow macaroni**
6 tablespoons	**unsalted butter,** divided
1/4 cup	**finely diced onion**
3 tablespoons	**flour**
3 cups	**whole milk**
1/2 teaspoon	**salt**
1/8 teaspoon	**pepper**
2 cups	**grated mild white cheddar cheese,** divided
1 cup	**grated fontina or Monterey Jack cheese,** divided
4	**Anaheim chiles,** roasted, peeled, seeded, diced
1 cup	**fresh breadcrumbs**

Preheat oven to 350 degrees. Prepare a 2-quart casserole dish with nonstick cooking spray. Cook macaroni in a large pot of boiling salted water to al dente, about 7 minutes; drain and set aside.

Melt 3 tablespoons butter over medium heat in a large saucepan. Add onion and saute until tender, about 5 minutes. Add flour and stir until flour is cooked but not brown, about 4 minutes. Gradually whisk milk into flour mixture and bring to a boil. Reduce heat, add salt and pepper, and simmer until thickened, about 8–10 minutes, stirring occasionally. Remove from heat. Mix cheeses together and add 3/4 of cheese mixture to the milk mixture; stir until cheese has melted.

Toss the macaroni and chiles together in a large bowl. Stir cheese sauce into macaroni and transfer to prepared dish. Top with remaining cheese. Melt remaining butter and toss with breadcrumbs; sprinkle evenly over top. Bake for 30 minutes, or until the cheese is bubbly and lightly browned. Makes 6 servings.

GREEN CHILE POTATO GRATIN

6	**russet potatoes**
3 cups	**heavy cream**
10 ounces	**Gruyere cheese,** grated
2	**Anaheim chiles,** roasted, peeled, diced **or 1 can (6 ounces) diced green chiles**
1 teaspoon	**salt**
1/2 teaspoon	**white pepper**
2 tablespoons	**minced fresh chives or cilantro,** for garnish
1–2	**green jalapenos,** sliced, for garnish
1–2	**red jalapenos or serrano chiles,** sliced, for garnish

Preheat oven to 375 degrees.

Peel potatoes and cut into 1/8-inch-thick slices (use a mandolin if possible so slices will be even and stack nicely). Butter a 9 x 13-inch baking dish. Layer potato slices neatly in the bottom of prepared dish. Spoon 5 tablespoons of heavy cream evenly over potatoes, and sprinkle sparingly with cheese and Anaheim chiles. Season with salt and pepper. Repeat layering process until potatoes, cream, cheese, and chiles are all used. Be sparing with cream and cheese so layers will stack nicely when cut and plated.

Press down on the potatoes to firmly stack them and to make sure they are covered in cream. Cover with aluminum foil and bake for 40 minutes. Remove foil and bake for another 30 minutes, until potatoes are fork tender and cream has been absorbed. Check potatoes 15 minutes before cooking time is finished. If potatoes are browning too quickly, replace the foil. When potatoes are tender, remove from oven and let rest for about 10–15 minutes. Slice into squares and garnish with chives, and sliced jalapenos, if desired. Makes 10–12 servings.

CHEDDAR-BACON GRITS

2 1/2 cups	**chicken stock**
2 cups	**whole milk**
I teaspoon	**salt**
I cup plus 2 tablespoons	**coarse-ground grits**
1/4 cup	**heavy cream**
2	**jalapenos,** roasted, peeled, seeded, minced
3/4 cup	**grated sharp cheddar cheese**
1/2 teaspoon	**pepper**
6 strips	**bacon,** cooked, crumbled
2 tablespoons	**thinly sliced green onions**

Bring chicken stock and milk to a boil in a large saucepan. Add salt. Slowly whisk grits into boiling stock, stirring constantly. Reduce heat to low and stir in cream. Cover and cook until liquid is absorbed and grits are creamy, about 20–25 minutes. Stir every few minutes to prevent grits from sticking to bottom of pan. Add jalapenos and cheese; stir until cheese is melted. Remove from heat. Season with pepper. Sprinkle bacon and green onions over grits and serve warm. Makes 6 servings.

CHILE POTATO STACKS

1 pound	**Yukon gold potatoes**
1 1/2 pounds	**Russet potatoes**
3 tablespoons	**Garlic-Chile Oil** (page 121)
3 tablespoons	**unsalted butter**
2 tablespoons	**fresh thyme leaves,** divided
2 teaspoons	**kosher salt,** divided
1/4 teaspoon	**freshly ground pepper**
3/4 cup	**finely grated Asiago cheese,** divided
1	**jalapeno,** seeded, minced

Preheat oven to 375 degrees. Prepare a 12-cup muffin pan with nonstick cooking spray.

Peel potatoes and keep in a bowl of cold water until ready to slice. Heat Garlic-Chile Oil, butter, 1 tablespoon thyme, 1 1/2 teaspoons salt, and pepper until butter has melted. Remove from heat and set aside.

Pat each potato dry and slice into rounds as thinly as possible using a mandolin with safety guard. Place potato slices in a large bowl.

Stir 1/2 cup cheese and jalapeno into chile oil mixture and pour over potatoes. Using your fingers, work mixture to coat each slice. Stack slices in prepared muffin cups. Sprinkle remaining cheese and salt over top. Bake until golden brown, about 45–50 minutes. Cool potatoes for 8 minutes. Remove from pan with a large spoon and garnish with remaining thyme before serving. Makes 12 servings.

HASSELBACK POTATOES ENCHILADA-STYLE

6	**small to medium russet potatoes**
½ cup	**Garlic-Chile Oil** (page 121)
6 strips	**bacon,** diced
1	**jalapeno, Anaheim, or Hatch chile,** seeded, minced
½ cup	**red chile sauce or enchilada sauce**
	salt and pepper, to taste
6 slices	**Monterey Jack cheese**
2 tablespoons	**minced fresh chives,** for garnish

Preheat oven to 425 degrees.

In a large saucepan, boil the potatoes with their skin on for 15 minutes, or until fork tender. Rinse in cool water until cool enough to handle.

Place the handle of a wooden spoon on each side of potato to use as a guide for cutting purposes. Starting at one end, make cuts across the potato ⅛ inch apart, stopping at the spoon handle. Do not cut through potato. Repeat for each potato.

Toss potatoes in Garlic-Chile Oil, working oil into cuts. Place in a large baking dish and sprinkle with bacon and minced chile. Bake for 10 minutes, until bacon begins to brown and crisp. Pour red chile sauce evenly over potatoes. Season with salt and pepper and top each potato with a slice of cheese. Bake until cheese is melted and bubbly, about 8–10 more minutes. Garnish with chives. Makes 6 servings.

SALSAS AND SAUCES

CLASSIC RED CHILE MOLE

2	**dried ancho chiles**
2	**dried guajillo chiles**
2	**dried pasilla or mulato chiles**
1/2 cup	**golden raisins**
	boiling water
1	**chipotle pepper in adobo**
1/4 cup	**almond butter**
2 ounces	**Mexican chocolate** (Ibarra or Abuelita), chopped
1	**jalapeno,** seeded
2	**medium yellow onions,** peeled and quartered
1 pound	**Roma tomatoes,** halved
3 tablespoons	**vegetable oil**
3 cloves	**garlic,** peeled
1/4 cup	**sesame seeds**
1 tablespoon	**black peppercorns**
1 stick	**Mexican canela or cinnamon,** broken in pieces
1 tablespoon	**dried Mexican oregano leaves**
2 teaspoons	**fresh thyme leaves or 1/2 teaspoon dried**
2 cups	**chicken stock**
1/2 teaspoon	**kosher salt**

Remove stems and seeds from dried chiles and cut into large pieces. Toast in a dry frying pan over low heat until fragrant. Place in a blender with raisins and enough boiling water to cover. Soak until softened, about 25 minutes. Add chipotle, almond butter, chocolate, and a few tablespoons of water, if needed, to make a smooth puree. Blend and then pour into a large saucepan.

Preheat oven to broil. In a large bowl, toss jalapeno, onions, and tomatoes in oil to coat. Spread on a baking sheet and roast until skins are bubbled and begin to char, about 5–7 minutes on each side, adding garlic halfway through. Remove from oven and allow to cool. Remove charred skins if desired and place roasted vegetables and garlic in blender; puree until smooth, and add to dried chile mixture.

Toast sesame seeds, peppercorns, canela, oregano, and thyme in a dry frying pan over low heat until fragrant. Grind in a spice grinder or blender and add to chile mixture.

Add stock to chile mixture and bring to a boil over medium-high heat. Add salt and simmer for 20–30 minutes, stirring occasionally. Serve as a sauce for enchiladas, chicken, or pork, or stir into braised beef for tacos and burritos. Makes 4 cups.

LAZY SUMMER SALSA

6	**medium Roma tomatoes,** halved
2–3	**jalapenos**
I	**medium yellow onion,** peeled, quartered
2 tablespoons	**vegetable oil**
	salt and pepper, to taste
4 cloves	**garlic,** peeled
½ cup	**vegetable or chicken stock**

Preheat oven to broil.

Place the tomato halves in a large mixing bowl. Cut the jalapenos in half, remove seeds and ribs, (if desired to cut the heat), and add to the tomatoes along with the onion. Toss with oil and place on a baking sheet with cut sides down; season with salt and pepper. Place baking sheet on top rack of oven and broil vegetables until skins are bubbled and begin to char, about 5–7 minutes on each side, adding garlic halfway through. Remove from oven and allow to cool for a few minutes.

Remove skins from tomatoes and jalapenos, if desired. Place roasted vegetables and garlic in a food processor or blender with stock and pulse into a chunky salsa. Pour salsa into a medium saucepan and heat to a simmer. Cook for 2–3 minutes. Season with salt and pepper.

Use Lazy Summer Salsa as a sauce for meats or enchiladas, or refrigerate and serve with chips. Store in refrigerator for up to I week. Makes 2½ cups.

RANCHERO SAUCE

1 1/2 pounds	**tomatillos,** husks removed
1	**small yellow onion,** peeled, quartered
2	**green New Mexico or Anaheim chiles,** seeded
2 tablespoons	**vegetable oil**
4 cloves	**garlic,** peeled
3 cups	**vegetable or chicken stock**
1 teaspoon	**cumin**
1/2	**lime,** juiced
1 teaspoon	**dried Mexican oregano leaves**
1 teaspoon	**salt**
1/2 teaspoon	**pepper**

Preheat oven to 450 degrees.

In a large bowl, toss tomatillos, onion, and chiles in oil to coat. Place on a baking sheet and roast in oven until skins are bubbled and begin to char, about 5–7 minutes on each side, adding garlic halfway through. Remove from oven and allow to cool.

Remove charred skins from tomatillos, onion, and chiles. Working in batches, place roasted vegetables and garlic in a blender with some of the stock and blend until smooth. Pour into a large saucepan, add cumin, remaining stock, lime juice, oregano, salt, and pepper. Bring to a simmer until sauce thickens, about 20 minutes. Serve with chile rellenos, chicken enchiladas, or omelets. Makes 4–5 cups.

AVOCADO-TOMATILLO SALSA

I pound	**tomatillos,** husks removed
I	**small white onion,** peeled, quartered
3	**jalapenos,** seeded
2 tablespoons	**vegetable oil**
3/4 cups	**water**
2	**large ripe avocados,** halved
2 tablespoons	**minced fresh cilantro**
1/2 teaspoon	**salt**
1/4 teaspoon	**pepper**

Preheat oven to 450 degrees.

In a large bowl, toss tomatillos, onion, and jalapenos in oil to coat. Place on a baking sheet and roast in oven until skins are bubbled and begin to char, about 5–7 minutes on each side. Remove from oven and allow to cool.

Remove charred skins from tomatillos, chiles, and onions. Place roasted vegetables and garlic in a blender, add water and avocados, and pulse until pureed but still chunky. Pour into a serving bowl and stir in cilantro, salt, and pepper. Chill before serving. Store in refrigerator for up to I week. Makes 2 1/2 cups.

SALSA VERDE

12	**tomatillos,** husks removed
4	**Anaheim chiles,** seeded
2	**serrano chiles or I jalapeno,** seeded
5 tablespoons	**vegetable oil,** divided
4 cloves	**garlic,** peeled
I cup	**diced yellow onion**
I cup	**chicken stock**
I teaspoon	**cumin**
I teaspoon	**salt**
$\frac{1}{2}$ teaspoon	**pepper**
I teaspoon	**lime juice**
$\frac{1}{3}$ cup	**chopped fresh cilantro**

Preheat oven to 450 degrees.

In a large bowl, toss tomatillos and chiles in 3 tablespoons of oil to coat. Place on a baking sheet and roast in oven until skins are bubbled and begin to char, about 5–7 minutes on each side, adding garlic halfway through. Remove from oven and allow to cool. Remove charred skins from tomatillos and chiles, place in a blender with the garlic, and puree until smooth.

Add remaining 2 tablespoons oil to a large frying pan and saute onion until soft and translucent, about 5 minutes. Stir in tomatillo puree, chicken stock, cumin, salt, pepper, lime juice, and cilantro. Simmer for 15 minutes.

Salsa Verde can be used in place of traditional red chile enchilada sauces with chicken, pork, enchiladas, seafood, and egg dishes. Makes 3 cups.

AUTHENTIC RED CHILE ENCHILADA SAUCE

4	**dried ancho chiles**
4	**dried guajillo chiles**
4	**dried New Mexico chiles**
4	**dried chiles de arbol**
1	**small onion,** peeled, quartered
2 cloves	**garlic,** peeled
2	**Roma tomatoes,** chopped
6 cups	**simmering water or chicken stock**
1 teaspoon	**dried Mexican oregano leaves**
1/4 teaspoon	**cumin**
	salt, to taste

Remove stems and seeds from chiles and cut into large pieces. Toast chiles, onion, and garlic in a dry frying pan over medium heat until fragrant, about 5 minutes.

Working in batches, fill blender halfway with chiles, onion, garlic, and tomatoes. Pour in enough water or stock to cover, and add oregano and cumin. Let sit for a few minutes to cool. Blend until very smooth. Strain mixture through a strainer or cheesecloth to remove pieces of dried chile. Repeat, if needed, until all vegetables have been blended. Place in a large saucepan and simmer for 25 minutes, stirring occasionally. Season with salt. Serve warm over enchiladas, burritos, or steaks. Makes 7–8 cups.

SOUTHWEST ENCHILADA SAUCE

¼ cup	**vegetable oil**
½ cup	**finely sliced onions**
1 tablespoon	**minced garlic**
½ cup	**New Mexico red chile powder**
2½ cups	**water or chicken stock**
½ teaspoon	**cumin**
1 teaspoon	**ground Mexican oregano**
¼ teaspoon	**salt**

Heat oil in a large saucepan over medium heat. Add onion and saute until soft, about 5 minutes. Add garlic and cook until onion is translucent, about more 2 minutes. Stir in chile powder and cook for 2 minutes. Add water, cumin, oregano, and salt.

Bring sauce to a boil, reduce heat, and simmer until thickened enough to coat the back of a spoon, about 20 minutes, stirring occasionally. Serve warm over enchiladas, burritos, and steaks. Makes about 3 cups.

TOMATILLO CREAM SAUCE

1 ½ pounds	**tomatillos,** husks removed
1	**jalapeno,** seeded
2 tablespoons	**vegetable oil,** divided
3 cups	**heavy cream**
2 tablespoons	**minced shallot**
2 cloves	**garlic,** peeled, minced
¼ cup	**white wine or chicken stock,** optional
½ cup	**sour cream**
	salt and white pepper, to taste

Preheat oven to 450 degrees.

In a large bowl, toss tomatillos and jalapeno in 1 tablespoon oil to coat. Place on a baking sheet and roast in oven until skins are bubbled and begin to char, about 5–7 minutes on each side. Remove from oven and allow to cool. Remove skins from tomatillos and jalapeno and puree in a blender until smooth; add a little of the heavy cream, if necessary.

Heat remaining oil in a large frying pan. Saute shallot and garlic until soft, about 2 minutes. Add wine. Reduce heat and simmer until liquid is almost gone. Stir in remaining heavy cream and sour cream. Simmer until slightly thickened; add tomatillo mixture and season with salt and pepper. Serve warm over enchiladas, steaks, seafood, or omelets. Makes about 5 cups.

CHIMICHURRI SALSA

1/4 cup	**chopped fresh cilantro**
1/2 cup	**chopped fresh parsley**
2 tablespoons	**finely chopped red onion**
2 tablespoons	**smashed, toasted pine nuts**
1/3 cup	**seasoned rice vinegar**
2 tablespoons	**olive oil**
1	**Fresno chile or jalapeno,** seeded, minced
	kosher salt and freshly ground pepper, to taste

In a small bowl, mix cilantro, parsley, onion, pine nuts, vinegar, oil, and chile together; season with salt and pepper. Keep in refrigerator, covered, for up to 1 week. Serve warm or cold on grilled meats or with seafood. Makes about 1 1/2 cups.

MAYAN-SPICED MANGO SAUCE

2	**large ripe mangoes,** peeled, diced
1	**large lime,** juiced
1	**habanero chile,** seeded
2 cloves	**garlic,** peeled, minced
4	**whole allspice berries,** toasted, crushed
1/4 teaspoon	**freshly ground pepper**
2 tablespoons	**achiote paste**
1/4 teaspoon	**cumin**
1 teaspoon	**dried Mexican oregano leaves**
1/4 teaspoon	**kosher salt**
2 tablespoons	**white vinegar**

Place diced mango in a blender or food processor with lime juice and habanero; puree until smooth but small pieces of mango remain. Add garlic, allspice, pepper, achiote paste, cumin, oregano, salt, and vinegar. Blend until well mixed. Cover and chill in refrigerator until ready to heat and serve. Use with Mayan-Spiced Grilled Pork Chops (page 52) or any of your favorite grilled meats. Makes about 2 cups.

DESSERTS

PEANUT BUTTER BOMBS

8	**dried chiles de arbol**
1/4 cup	**sugar**
24	**Hershey's Kisses,** wrappers removed
1/2 cup	**unsalted butter**
1 cup	**firmly packed light brown sugar**
1	**egg,** beaten
1 teaspoon	**vanilla**
1 cup	**creamy peanut butter**
1 1/2 cups	**flour**
1 teaspoon	**baking soda**
1/4 teaspoon	**salt**
1 cup	**chopped roasted, salted peanuts**

Toast whole chiles in a dry frying pan over low heat until fragrant.
When cooled remove stems and seeds and grind into a powder using a
spice grinder or blender. Mix sugar and chile powder together in a small
bowl. Cut the tip off each Hershey's Kiss and press firmly into sugar
mixture to coat evenly. Set aside.

In a large bowl, cream butter and brown sugar together until fluffy. Add
egg, vanilla, and peanut butter; beat until well combined. In a separate
bowl, stir together the flour, baking soda, and salt. Add flour to peanut
butter mixture and beat on low to combine; mix in peanuts. Cover and
chill in refrigerator for 2–4 hours.

Preheat oven to 350 degrees. Prepare a large baking sheet with
parchment paper or nonstick cooking spray.

Scoop 2 tablespoons of dough and press into the palm of your hand.
Place a Hershey's Kiss in the center of the dough and seal dough
around the chocolate, rolling into a ball. Press top of each cookie into
remaining chile powder mixture. Place on prepared baking sheet. Bake
15–18 minutes or until golden brown. Serve warm. Makes 2 dozen.

AZTEC CHOCOLATE CREAM PIE

1	**dried ancho, pasillo, or mulato chile**
1 cup	**boiling water**
3 boxes (5 ounces each)	**Heat and Serve Chocolate Pudding Mix**
9 cups	**whole milk**
1 stick	**butter,** cubed
4 (1.55 ounces each)	**Hershey's Milk Chocolate Bars,** broken into pieces
½ teaspoon	**salt**
2	**prepared Graham Cracker-Pecan Pie Crusts** (page 114)
2 cups	**heavy whipping cream**
⅓ cup	**powdered sugar**
1 ½ teaspoons	**vanilla**

Remove stem and seeds from chile, chop into large pieces, and toast in a dry frying pan over low heat until fragrant, making sure it doesn't burn. Place chile in a small bowl and cover with boiling water. Soak for 25–30 minutes until rehydrated. Place chile in a blender with 1 tablespoon of the soaking water and blend to make a paste. Press paste through a sieve to catch any pieces of chile. Set aside.

Pour pudding mix into a large saucepan and slowly whisk in milk until there are no lumps. Add chile paste and cook over medium heat until pudding comes to a boil, stirring constantly. Remove from heat as soon as it begins to boil. Quickly stir in butter, chocolate, and salt until melted and well combined. Pour pudding into pie crusts and cover each pie with plastic wrap. Plastic wrap should touch surface of pudding to prevent a skin from forming. Refrigerate until chilled.

In a large bowl, whip cream until it begins to thicken. Add powdered sugar and vanilla and continue to whip until medium peaks form. Divide whipped cream between the pies, spreading evenly over top; refrigerate to set whipped cream. Makes 2 pies.

GRILLED MANGO WITH HONEY AND PISTACHIOS

3	**dried chiles de arbol**
3 tablespoons	**water**
4 tablespoons	**mesquite honey**
3	**large, ripe mangoes**
6–12 (8–12 inch)	**bamboo skewers,** soaked in water
2–3 tablespoons	**chopped pistachios**
$\frac{1}{2}$ teaspoon	**New Mexico red chile powder**
$\frac{1}{2}$ teaspoon	**salt**
1	**large lime,** cut into wedges

Remove stems and seeds from chiles and chop into large pieces. Toast in a dry frying pan over low heat until fragrant. When cooled, grind in a spice grinder or blender to make chile flakes. Make a simple syrup by mixing water, chile flakes, and honey together in the same pan. Bring to a boil and immediately remove from heat; set aside.

Cut large cheeks (the fattest part) off of each side of mangoes. Peel each mango cheek and cut into large cubes (usually 6 cubes per cheek, depending upon the size of the mango). Place 4 to 6 cubes on each skewer. If mangoes are very ripe, use 2 skewers per serving to stabilize fruit for grilling.

Preheat grill or grill pan to medium-high heat. Grill mangoes until grill marks appear. If the mangoes are soft and very ripe, only grill one side. Try to grill mangoes quickly, or on high heat, so they do not become too soft.

Place skewers on a serving platter, drizzle with honey syrup, and sprinkle with pistachios, chile powder, and salt. Serve with lime wedges as a side dish or over ice cream. Makes 4–6 servings.

FIERY CHOCOLATE-DIPPED STRAWBERRIES

20	**large strawberries,** with stems
2	**dried chiles de arbol**
½ cup	**sugar**
½ teaspoon	**cinnamon**
½ cup	**semisweet chocolate chips**
2 tablespoons	**heavy cream**

Rinse strawberries and pat dry. Line a baking sheet or large platter with parchment or waxed paper.

Toast whole chiles in a dry frying pan over low heat until fragrant. When cooled remove stems and seeds, tear into pieces, and grind in a spice grinder or blender to make a powder.

In a small bowl, mix chile powder, sugar, and cinnamon together; set aside.

Heat chocolate and cream together in a double boiler. When melted, stir until smooth and shiny. Hold strawberries near stem and dip in chocolate, allowing excess chocolate to drip off. Set berries on prepared baking sheet or platter. Sprinkle berries with chile sugar or dip one corner or one side of berries into chile sugar. Let chocolate set before serving. Makes 20 strawberries.

Note: If you toast the chiles with the seeds and seed ball intact, it add to the heat of the chile.

MEXICAN ROCKY ROAD ICE CREAM

4	**eggs**
1/4 cup	**sweetened condensed milk**
4	**dried ancho chiles**
2 cups	**heavy cream**
1 cup plus 2 tablespoons	**half-and-half**
1/2 teaspoon	**Mexican cinnamon**
1 teaspoon	**cocoa powder**
1	**pinch kosher salt**
1 1/2 disks	**Mexican chocolate** (Ibarra or Abuelita), chopped
2/3 cup	**chopped toasted almonds**
2/3 cup	**mini marshmallows**

Crack the eggs into a large bowl and mix with the condensed milk, beating until well combined. Set aside.

Remove stems and seeds from chiles and chop into large pieces. Toast in a large saucepan until fragrant, about 4 minutes. Add the cream, half-and-half, cinnamon, cocoa powder, and salt. Bring to a boil over medium-high heat. Reduce heat and add the chocolate, stirring until melted. Remove pan from heat.

Slowly pour cream mixture through a fine sieve into egg mixture, whisking quickly until smooth. Refrigerate until completely cooled, about 2–4 hours, then freeze in ice cream maker according to manufacturer's instructions.

When ice cream is almost set, stir in the almonds and marshmallows. Pour into a container and finish setting ice cream in freezer. Makes 6 1/2 cups.

SPICY CANDIED NUTS

2 cups	**pecan halves**
2 tablespoons	**butter**
1/4 cup	**sugar**
2 tablespoons	**grated piloncillo or brown sugar**
1 teaspoon	**New Mexico red chile powder**
1 teaspoon	**cinnamon**
1/2 teaspoon	**ground ginger**

Prepare a large baking sheet with parchment paper or nonstick cooking spray.

Toast pecans in a dry frying pan over medium-high heat until fragrant and lightly brown, about 4 minutes. Stir frequently. Add butter and stir until melted. Add sugars and spices. Stir and cook until sugar caramelizes and coats pecans. Remove from pan and spread on prepared baking sheet; cool. Store in an airtight container for up to 1 week. Use in dessert recipes, salads, or as a snack. Makes 2 cups.

RASPBERRY RED CHILE SORBET

I quart	**frozen raspberries**
I tablespoon	**minced chipotle pepper in adobo, Fresno chile, or serrano chile,** seeded
¾ cup	**sugar**
¾ cup	**water**
I	**lemon,** juiced

Put raspberries and chile in food processor or blender. Process into a puree and pour through a strainer. Discard any remaining solids. Place puree in a bowl and chill.

Make a simple syrup by mixing sugar and water together in a small saucepan. Bring to a boil and simmer until sugar is dissolved, about 3 minutes. Remove from heat, transfer to a medium bowl, and chill.

Mix the raspberry puree and simple syrup mixture together and add the lemon juice. Chill completely in refrigerator. Once the mixture has chilled, transfer to ice cream maker and process according to manufacturer's directions. Makes 4–5 cups.

GREEN CHILE
APPLE CROSTATA

3	**small Granny Smith apples**
I tablespoon	**lemon juice**
¼ cup	**diced roasted Hatch or Anaheim chiles**
¼ cup plus I tablespoon	**sugar,** divided
I teaspoon	**cinnamon**
⅛ teaspoon	**nutmeg**
I pinch	**salt**
2 tablespoons	**cornstarch**
I (12-inch)	**unbaked pie crust**
I	**egg**
I tablespoon	**water**

Preheat oven to 400 degrees. Prepare a large baking sheet with parchment paper or nonstick cooking spray.

Peel apples and slice into ⅛-inch-thick slices. Place apple slices in a large bowl, and toss with lemon juice and chiles. In a separate bowl, stir together ¼ cup sugar, cinnamon, nutmeg, salt, and cornstarch; add to apple mixture and toss to coat.

Place pie crust on prepared baking sheet. Place apple mixture in the center of the pie crust, leaving a 2-inch border around the apples. Fold crust up and over the edges of the apples to form an 8-inch round crostata. In a small bowl, beat the egg and water together and brush over crust; sprinkle crust with remaining I tablespoon sugar.

Bake until apples are tender and crust is golden brown, about 30–45 minutes. Makes 6 servings.

MEXICAN CHOCOLATE BROWNIES

2	**dried ancho, pasilla, or mulato chiles**
I cup	**boiling water**
10 ounces	**semisweet chocolate chips**
10 ounces	**Mexican chocolate** (Ibarra or Abuelita), chopped
3 sticks	**butter**
5	**eggs**
I cup plus 2 tablespoons	**sugar**
I tablespoon	**vanilla**
I cup	**flour**
$^1/_2$ tablespoon	**baking powder**
2 teaspoons	**cinnamon**
$^1/_2$ teaspoon	**salt**
$^1/_2$ teaspoon	**cayenne pepper**
I $^1/_2$ cups	**chopped toasted walnuts,** optional

Remove stem and seeds from chile, chop, and toast chile pieces in a dry frying pan over low heat until fragrant. Place in a small bowl and cover with water. Soak for 25–30 minutes until rehydrated. Place chile pieces in a blender with I tablespoon of the soaking water and puree to make a paste. Press paste through a sieve; set aside.

Preheat oven to 350 degrees. Grease a 9 x 13-inch baking pan and dust with flour. Melt chocolates and butter together in a double boiler; remove from heat and cool. In a large bowl, beat eggs, sugar, chile paste, and vanilla together. Whisk in cooled chocolate mixture to combine. In a separate bowl, mix together the flour, baking powder, cinnamon, salt, and cayenne pepper; stir into chocolate. Whisk until smooth. Fold in walnuts. Pour batter into prepared pan, smooth top, and bake for 25–30 minutes, or until a toothpick inserted in the center comes out clean. Makes I6 brownies.

MAYAN TRUFFLES

½ cup	**heavy cream**
2 teaspoons	**ancho chile powder**
10 ounces	**semisweet chocolate chips**
6 ounces	**bittersweet chocolate,** chopped
1 teaspoon	**vanilla or strong coffee**
2 tablespoons	**butter**
¼ cup	**cocoa powder**
1 cup	**turbinado or raw sugar**
2 tablespoons	**cinnamon**

Line the sides and bottom of an 8 x 8-inch baking pan with plastic wrap.

Whisk almond milk and chile powder together in a double boiler and heat until bubbles appear along the sides of the pan. Turn off heat. Add both chocolates and stir until melted and smooth. Remove from stove and stir in vanilla and butter. Pour chocolate mixture into prepared pan. Cover chocolate with plastic wrap, making sure it touches the surface of the chocolate. Refrigerate for 3 hours or overnight. When ready to roll truffles, uncover the chocolate and invert on counter covered with parchment paper. Cut the chocolate into 1-inch squares. Dust hands with a little cocoa powder and roll the squares into balls.

Mix the sugar and cinnamon together in a shallow bowl. Roll truffle balls in sugar cinnamon mix and place on a parchment-lined tray. Chill until set, about 30 minutes. Refrigerate truffles in an airtight container for up to 2 weeks. Bring to room temperature before serving. Makes about 50–60 truffles.

Note: If you prefer a spicier flavor, substitute 2 teaspoons chile de arbol powder for the ancho chile powder.

CHURROS WITH CHILE SUGAR

2	**dried chiles de arbol**
I teaspoon	**cinnamon**
1/2 cup	**sugar**
I cup	**milk**
1/2 cup	**unsalted butter**
1/4 teaspoon	**salt**
I cup	**flour**
3	**eggs**
	vegetable oil, for frying
I cup	**Mayan Chocolate Ganache**
	(page 94)

Toast chiles in a dry frying pan over low heat until fragrant, about 2 minutes. Remove stems and seeds. Grind to a powder in a spice grinder or blender. In a small bowl, stir together the chile powder, cinnamon, and sugar; pour onto a plate and set aside.

In a medium saucepan, bring milk, butter, and salt to a boil over medium-high heat. Stir in flour. Reduce heat to low and continue to stir constantly until dough pulls away from side of pan, about 3 minutes. Transfer dough to a mixing bowl and mix on low speed for I minute. Beat eggs into dough one at a time at medium speed. Transfer dough to a large pastry bag with a large open star tip.

Heat 2 inches of oil to 360 degrees in a large, deep saucepan. Pipe dough into hot oil in 4-inch strips, and fry to a golden brown, about 4 minutes. Remove from oil, drain on paper towels, and roll in sugar mixture while still hot. Serve warm with Mayan Chocolate Ganache. Makes 16 churros.

MEXICAN CHOCOLATE-WALNUT FUDGE

3 (4½ ounces each)	**Hershey's Chocolate Bars**
1 bag (12 ounces)	**semisweet chocolate chips**
1 jar (7 ounces)	**marshmallow cream**
2 tablespoons	**butter**
1 tablespoon	**ancho chile powder**
½ teaspoon	**cinnamon**
4½ cups	**sugar**
1 can (12 ounces)	**evaporated milk**
1 pound	**walnuts,** toasted, chopped
1 teaspoon	**vanilla**

Chop chocolate bars and place in a large bowl. Add chocolate chips, marshmallow cream, and butter. Set aside.

In a large saucepan, combine chile powder, cinnamon, sugar, and evaporated milk. Bring to a boil then boil for exactly 6 minutes. Pour over chocolate mixture and stir until just smooth. Do not overstir. Stir in walnuts and vanilla. Spoon into mounds on buttered wax paper to cool. Makes 18 pieces.

Note: If you prefer a spicier flavor, substitute 1 tablespoon chile de arbol powder for the ancho chile powder.

MAYAN CHOCOLATE GANACHE

8 ounces	**heavy cream**
¼ teaspoon	**chipotle or New Mexico red chile powder**
2 disks (3 ounces each)	**Mexican chocolate** (Ibarra or Abuelita), chopped
3 ounces	**semisweet chocolate,** chopped
1 tablespoon	**unsalted butter**
⅛ teaspoon	**salt**

In a medium saucepan over medium-high heat, stir together the cream and chile powder until scalded, or small bubbles appear around the sides of the pan. Remove pan from heat and add both chocolates. Let sit for 4 minutes for chocolate to melt then stir until completely smooth. Stir in butter and salt. Allow ganache to cool. Use as a frosting for cake or as a dipping sauce. Makes 2 cups.

MEXICAN CHOCOLATE-PECAN CAKE

1 ½ cups	**whole pecans**
1 ½ cups	**sugar,** divided
¾ cup	**flour**
½ teaspoon	**salt**
2 ounces	**semisweet chocolate,** chopped
2 ounces	**unsweetened chocolate,** chopped
8 tablespoons	**unsalted butter,** cubed
2 tablespoons	**sarsaparilla or root beer**
2 tablespoons	**ancho chile powder**
8	**egg whites**
1 recipe	**Mayan Chocolate Ganache** (page 94)

Preheat oven to 350 degrees. Prepare a 9 x 9-inch cake pan with nonstick cooking spray and dust with flour. Cover bottom of pan with waxed or parchment paper and spray paper with cooking spray.

Pulse pecans and ¾ cup sugar in a food processor until finely ground. Place mixture into a mixing bowl, and stir in flour and salt. Melt chocolates and butter in a double boiler until smooth. Remove from heat. Stir in sarsaparilla and chile powder; set aside.

In a medium bowl, beat egg whites until soft peaks form. Gradually add remaining ¾ cup sugar, and beat until it holds a soft peak. Do not overbeat into firm peaks. Fold in pecan mixture. Gently fold chocolate mixture into egg whites. Pour into prepared pan and bake for 45–50 minutes, or until a toothpick inserted into the center comes out clean. Loosen sides of cake from pan and cool on wire rack for 5–10 minutes. When cool, turn cake out of pan and remove paper. Once cake is completely cooled, pour warm ganache over top and down the sides. Makes 9 servings.

ORANGE POLENTA CAKE

I cup	**fine polenta or corn meal**
⅔ cup	**whole milk**
I heaping tablespoon	**orange zest**
¾ cup	**sugar**
¾ cup	**flour**
I teaspoon	**salt**
I teaspoon	**baking powder**
2	**large eggs**
I	**egg yolk**
½ cup	**extra virgin olive oil**
¼ cup	**honey**
I recipe	**Orange Habanero Glaze** (page 97)
	whipped cream and orange slices, for garnish

Preheat oven to 350 degrees. Grease a 9-inch round cake pan and dust with flour.

Place polenta into a food processor and pulse to a fine grind. Pour into a medium bowl. Heat milk in a small saucepan until little bubbles appear around the edge. Pour milk over the polenta and stir. Set aside to allow polenta to soften.

In a small bowl, mix together zest and sugar; set aside. In a large bowl, sift flour, salt, and baking powder together. In a separate bowl, beat eggs, egg yolk, oil, and honey together until frothy. Add the polenta mixture and sugar mixture to the eggs; stir to combine. Add egg mixture to flour and beat for 2 minutes. Do not overbeat. Pour batter into prepared pan and bake for 35–45 minutes, or until a toothpick inserted into the center comes out clean. Remove from oven and cool for about 10 minutes. Remove from pan to a serving plate. Pour glaze over cake while it is still warm to the touch but not hot. Garnish with whipped cream and orange slices. Makes 6–8 servings.

ORANGE-HABANERO GLAZE

½ cup **orange juice**
I heaping tablespoon **orange zest**
I **habanero chile,** seeded, finely minced
2 cups **powdered sugar**

In a microwave-safe bowl, heat orange juice in microwave until just about to boil, approximately 90 seconds. Add the orange zest and minced chile and stir. Let sit about 15 minutes, to infuse flavors.

Add sugar to orange juice mixture and stir until no lumps are left. Taste test glaze on a bit of bread to see if more chile needs to be added. Makes about I cup.

RASPBERRY-CHIPOTLE DONUT BITES

2	**dried chiles de arbol**
½ cup	**sugar**
I teaspoon	**cinnamon**
I2 pieces	**frozen dinner roll dough**
	vegetable oil, for frying
I cup	**Raspberry-Chipotle Jam** (page I23) **or store-bought jam,** mixed with I teaspoon **New Mexico red chile powder**

Toast chiles in a dry frying pan over low heat until fragrant. Remove stems and seeds, tear into pieces, and grind to a powder in a spice grinder or blender. In a small bowl, mix together the chile powder, sugar, and cinnamon; set aside.

Thaw dough according to package directions. Cut rolls into three pieces while soft but still cold. Reshape pieces into balls. Place on a baking sheet and let rise until doubled in size. Heat 2 inches of oil to 360 degrees in a large, deep saucepan. Fry dough in hot oil until lightly golden, about 3 minutes. Remove from oil and roll in sugar mixture.

Place jam in a piping bag with a small round tip. Press tip into donuts and squeeze a little jam into the center. Roll in sugar again, if necessary. Makes 36 donut bites.

Variation: Once the donut bites are filled, dip them in Orange-Habanero Glaze (page 97) instead of the chile sugar.

STRAWBERRY LIMEADE POPSICLES

3	**dried chiles de arbol**
I pound	**fresh strawberries**
I	**large lime,** juiced (about 2–3 tablespoons)
I cup plus 2 tablespoons	**sugar,** divided
I cup	**plain yogurt**
I cup	**coconut milk**
¼ teaspoon	**vanilla,** optional

Toast chiles in a dry frying pan over low heat until fragrant. Remove stems and seeds, tear into pieces, and grind into powder in a spice grinder or blender. Set aside.

Wash Popsicle molds and place in the freezer along with sticks to chill.

Wash strawberries and remove stems, cutting larger berries in half so that all are similar in size. Place in the bowl of a food processor and pulse until berries are finely diced (not pureed). Add lime juice, ½ cup sugar, and chile powder; stir to combine. Set aside. In a medium bowl, combine the yogurt, coconut milk, and remaining sugar. Add vanilla.

Remove molds from freezer and layer 2 spoonfuls of strawberry mixture into the bottom of each mold. Carefully pour I inch or so of coconut mixture over berries. Repeat layers until molds are filled. Add sticks and tops of molds and place in freezer for 6–8 hours or overnight. Makes 10 Popsicles.

FLOURLESS CHOCOLATE-CHILE CAKE

I	**large dried ancho, pasilla, or mulato chile**
I cup	**boiling water**
I cup plus 2 tablespoons	**unsalted butter,** divided
4 ounces	**Mexican chocolate** (Ibarra or Abuelita), chopped
4 ounces	**bittersweet chocolate,** chopped
¼ cup	**unsweetened cocoa powder**
½ teaspoon	**cinnamon**
½ teaspoon	**salt**
6	**eggs,** separated
I cup	**sugar,** divided
	powdered sugar, for garnish
	whipped cream, for serving

Remove stem and seeds from chile, chop, and toast chile pieces in a dry frying pan over low heat until fragrant. Place in a small bowl and cover with boiling water. Soak for 25–30 minutes until rehydrated. Remove chile pieces to a blender and puree with I tablespoon of the soaking water to make a smooth paste. Press paste through a sieve; set aside.

Preheat oven to 350 degrees. Using 2 tablespoons of butter, grease the sides and bottom of a 9-inch springform pan and line bottom of pan with buttered parchment.

Melt both chocolates and I cup butter over medium-low heat in a double boiler until smooth; remove from heat. Whisk in cocoa powder, chile paste, cinnamon, and salt.

In a medium bowl, whip egg whites until thick and foamy. Slowly add ½ cup sugar and beat to medium peaks. Set aside.

In a separate bowl, beat egg yolks and remaining 1/2 cup sugar until pale yellow and thickened. Gradually stir chocolate mixture into egg yolks. Gently fold 1/3 of the egg whites into chocolate mixture until well incorporated. Gently fold in the remaining 2/3 egg whites in 2 batches. Do not overmix and deflate the egg whites.

Pour into prepared pan and bake for about 45 minutes, or until edges are set and center is still moist. Remove from oven and place on a wire rack until completely cooled. Run a knife around the edges and remove sides of pan. Transfer cake onto serving dish and gently lift cake with a spatula. Remove parchment from bottom of cake. Dust with powdered sugar and serve with whipped cream, if desired. Makes 8–12 servings.

MANGO-HABANERO POPSICLES

2 cups	**sugar**
1 cup	**water**
6 cups	**fresh or frozen mango chunks**
4 tablespoons	**pineapple juice**
1/4 teaspoon	**salt**
1–2	**habanero chiles,** seeded
2 tablespoons	**New Mexico red chile powder**
1 tablespoon	**salt**

Pour sugar into a medium saucepan. Carefully add water without splashing sugar onto sides of pan. Do not stir. Bring to a simmer over medium heat. Immediately turn down heat and lightly simmer for 5 minutes to thicken (do not allow sugar to caramelize or turn color). Syrup should be as clear as possible. Pour into a heatproof bowl to cool. Set aside.

Place mangoes in a food processor. Add pineapple juice, salt, and habaneros. Process into a very smooth puree. Add 1/2 of the simple syrup and taste for sweetness, adding more as needed. The mango puree should be sweet but retain its tartness. Chill puree 6–8 hours or overnight. Pour into Popsicle molds, add sticks and tops, and freeze.

In a small bowl, mix chile powder and salt together. Remove Popsicles from molds and dip one corner of each Popsicle into chile powder mixture before serving. Makes 8–10 Popsicles.

ORANGE-HABANERO CREME BRULEE

4 cups	**heavy cream**
1 ½ cups	**sugar,** divided
1	**habanero chile,** seeded, halved
1	**vanilla bean,** split lengthwise
	zest of 2 oranges
7	**egg yolks**
¼ teaspoon	**kosher salt**
	boiling water

Preheat oven to 325 degrees. Prepare 6 (7 ounces each) ramekins with nonstick cooking spray.

In a saucepan over medium-high heat, combine cream, ½ cup sugar, and chile. Scrape the seeds from the vanilla bean into the pan and add the vanilla pod; bring to a boil. Remove from heat. Cover pan and let steep for 10 minutes. Remove and discard chiles and vanilla bean.

Whisk ¼ cup sugar, orange zest, egg yolks, and salt together in a medium bowl until yolks are light in color. While whisking, add flavored cream mixture to egg mixture a little at a time until fully incorporated. Ladle evenly into prepared ramekins, and then place ramekins in a roasting pan. Pour enough boiling water into pan to come halfway up the sides of the ramekins. Bake for 40–45 minutes, until set but center still jiggles. Remove ramekins from roasting pan and chill in the refrigerator. When ready to serve, sprinkle remaining ¾ cup sugar evenly over the surface of each dish. If using a kitchen torch, melt the sugar until brown and bubbly to form a crispy top. If using an oven, set ramekins on a baking sheet and set on top rack under preheated boiler. Broil for 1–2 minutes, or until sugar is melted and bubbling. Makes 6 servings.

BEVERAGES, CONDIMENTS, AND GARNISHES

CHILE LEMONADE

1 ½ cups	**fresh lemon juice** (about 10 lemons)
1 cup	**sugar**
2 cups	**water**
1 tablespoon	**chile powder**
1 tablespoon	**kosher salt**
1	**lime,** cut into 6 wedges
3	**lemons,** thinly sliced
2	**green Anaheim chiles,** seeded, thinly sliced

Strain lemon juice through a sieve into a pitcher. Add sugar and stir until it dissolves. Pour in water.

Mix chile powder and salt together on a small plate. Moisten rim of each serving glass with a lime wedge, dip rim of glass in chile powder, and twist to coat.

Place 1–2 lemon slices and 1–2 chile slices in the bottom of each glass. Smash them a little with the end of a wooden spoon. Fill glasses with ice. Pour lemonade into glasses and serve with a slice of lemon and a slice of chile on the rim of the glass. Makes 6 servings.

MEHICAN HOT CHOCOLATE

1	**dried chile de arbol**
2	**dried ancho chiles**
4 cups	**milk**
1	**vanilla bean,** split down center
6 ounces	**Mexican chocolate** (Ibarra
	or Abuelita), chopped
1 cup	**whipped cream**
	cinnamon, for garnish

Remove stems from chiles. Split chiles in half lengthwise, remove seeds, and open flat. Toast chiles in a large saucepan until fragrant. Add milk and vanilla bean, scraping seeds into the pan; bring to a simmer. Remove from heat, cover, and steep for 15–20 minutes. Remove and discard chiles and vanilla bean. Return pan to heat and bring to a simmer over medium heat.

Add chocolate to simmering milk and stir until melted and smooth. Serve with a dollop of whipped cream and a dash of cinnamon. Makes 6 servings.

CAFE OLE (COFFEE WITH MEXICAN CHOCOLATE)

I	**dried ancho chile**
I	**dried chile de arbol**
¾ cup	**dark roast ground coffee**
2 teaspoons	**cinnamon,** plus extra for garnish
6 cups	**water**
I cup	**milk**
2 tablespoons	**turbinado or raw sugar**
3 ounces	**Mexican chocolate** (Ibarra or Abuelita), chopped
I teaspoon	**vanilla**
	whipped cream, for serving

Remove stem and seeds from chiles and tear into pieces. Place coffee, cinnamon, and chile pieces in the filter basket of coffeemaker. Add water and brew.

Bring milk and sugar to a simmer in a small saucepan over medium heat, stirring to dissolve sugar. Turn off heat and add chocolate. Stir until melted and smooth. Stir milk mixture into coffee and add vanilla. Serve with whipped cream, if desired. Makes 6–8 cups.

EL TOREADOR MOCKTAIL

	ice cubes
3 tablespoons	**Hershey's Chocolate Syrup**
I teaspoon	**ancho chile powder**
$1/8$ teaspoon	**cinnamon**
$1/2$ cup	**half-and-half**
16 ounces	**club soda,** chilled
I pinch	**cayenne pepper**

Put ice cubes in a cocktail shaker. Add chocolate syrup, ancho chile powder, cinnamon, and half-and-half; shake well. Add club soda, shaking lightly to mix. Pour into chilled glasses and top with cayenne pepper. Makes 2 servings.

BLOODY MARIA MOCKTAIL

1 ½ teaspoons	**kosher salt**
1 ½ teaspoons	**New Mexico red chile powder,** divided
1	**lime wedge**
	ice cubes
2 tablespoons	**lime juice**
½ cup	**club soda**
1 ½ cups	**tomato juice**
1 teaspoon	**grated horseradish**
1 teaspoon	**Worcestershire Sauce**
1 teaspoon	**lime zest**
	jicama spears, cucumber spears, and celery stalks, for garnish

Mix salt and ½ teaspoon chile powder together on a small plate. Moisten rims of 2 tall chilled glasses with juice from lime wedge, dip rim into chile mixture, and twist to coat. Fill glasses with ice and set aside.

Mix remaining 1 teaspoon chile powder with lime juice, club soda, tomato juice, horseradish, Worcestershire sauce, and lime zest in a small pitcher and pour into glasses. Garnish with jicama, cucumber, and celery. Makes 2 servings.

MANGO-HABANERO LIQUADO

2 cups	**almond milk**
I cup	**diced mango**
$1/2$	**banana**
I–2	**habanero chiles,** seeded
I tablespoon	**honey**
I teaspoon	**almond extract**
I cup	**ice cubes**

Pour almond milk into a blender and add remaining ingredients. Blend until smooth. Serve in chilled glasses. Makes 2 servings.

CHERRY BOMB LIMEADE

⅔ cup	**sugar**
⅔ cup	**water**
2	**jalapenos,** seeded, sliced
5	**limes,** juiced, chilled
1 ½	**cups pure cherry juice,** chilled
2 cups	**club soda,** chilled
	ice cubes
	lime wedges, for garnish

Combine sugar and water in a medium saucepan over medium-high heat and stir until sugar is dissolved. Bring water to a boil then remove from heat and cool.

Place jalapeno slices in the bottom of a pitcher. Pour sugar water into pitcher and chill. Add chilled lime juice, cherry juice, and club soda to pitcher. Taste limeade. If limeade is spicy enough, remove jalapenos or leave them in pitcher to increase heat level.

Pour cherry limeade over ice in chilled glasses and garnish with lime wedges. Makes 5–6 servings.

CHILE-LIME VINAIGRETTE

2	**limes,** zested
¼ cup	**lime juice** (about 4 limes)
2 tablespoons	**red chile powder**
½ cup	**honey**
2 tablespoons	**water**
	salt and pepper, to taste

In a small bowl, combine lime zest, juice, and chile powder. Stir in honey and water. Season with salt and pepper. Makes about 1 cup.

GRAHAM CRACKER-PECAN PIE CRUST

9 ounces	**graham crackers** (about 18 full crackers)
1/3 cup	**chopped pecans**
1/2 cup	**sugar**
1/2 teaspoon	**cinnamon**
1/2 teaspoon	**ancho chile powder**
1/2 teaspoon	**salt**
8 tablespoons	**butter,** melted

Working in small batches, break graham crackers into dime-sized pieces and place 1/4–1/2 of cracker pieces into a food processor. Pulse until crackers are size of large, grains of sand. Pour into a large mixing bowl and repeat with remaining crackers. Do not overprocess. There may still be larger pieces that can be broken up by hand.

Toast chopped pecans in a hot frying pan over medium-high heat just until fragrant. Pulse in food processor until same size as cracker crumbs. Add to cracker crumbs. Mix in the sugar, cinnamon, chile powder, and salt.

Drizzle melted butter evenly over crumb mixture while stirring. Continue stirring until crumbs are moistened. Divide mixture between 2, 10-inch pie plates. Reserve about 1 cup to fill holes in crusts, if needed. Use the bottom of a measuring cup to press mixture evenly into the bottom and up the sides of the pie plates. The crust should be about 1/4-inch thick. Place crusts in refrigerator to chill. Makes 2, 10-inch pie shells.

CANDIED JALAPENOS

¾ cup **water**
I cup **apple cider vinegar**
I cup **sugar**
6 **jalapenos**

Mix water, vinegar, and sugar together in a medium saucepan. Bring to a simmer and stir until sugar has dissolved, about 2–3 minutes.

Slice jalapenos into ¼-inch-thick slices. Add jalapeno slices to sugar mixture and simmer until jalapenos begin to soften, about 3–4 minutes. Remove jalapenos with a slotted spoon and place in a 16-ounce jar to cool. Continue to boil sugar mixture for another 4–5 minutes to reduce liquid. Pour over jalapenos. Place lid tightly on jar and store in refrigerator for up to 2 weeks. Use Candied Jalapenos in salads, coleslaw, sandwiches, or desserts. Makes I (16-ounce) jar.

TRES CHILES SPICE RUB

1 tablespoon	**pure guajillo or New Mexico red chile powder**
1 ½ teaspoons	**chipotle chile powder**
1 teaspoon	**ancho chile powder**
3 teaspoons	**smoked paprika**
1 ½ teaspoons	**cumin**
½ teaspoon	**onion powder**
½ teaspoon	**garlic powder**
1 teaspoon	**salt**
½ teaspoon	**pepper**

Mix chile powders and spices together in an airtight container. Use on fish, chicken, and meats, or sprinkle on anything that needs a little kick. Makes about ¼ cup.

CHIPOTLE SOUR CREAM

1	**chipotle pepper in adobo**
1 cup	**sour cream**
½ teaspoon	**kosher salt**
1 pinch	**pepper**

Remove stem and seeds, if any, from chipotle; mince. Mix half of minced chipotle into sour cream and taste. Add more chipotle if more heat is desired. Stir in salt and pepper.

For smoky chipotle flavor but less heat, use 1 tablespoon of the adobo sauce instead of the chipotle pepper. Makes 1 cup.

GREEN CHILE PESTO

1	**large poblano chile,** roasted
1	**large Anaheim chile,** roasted
4 cloves	**garlic,** peeled, sliced
1/4 cup	**chopped toasted pine nuts, cashews, or walnuts**
1/4 cup	**chopped fresh basil, cilantro, or parsley**
1/4 cup	**fresh grated Parmesan cheese**
1/4 teaspoon	**cumin**
1/8 cup	**lime or lemon juice**
1/4–1/2 cup	**light olive oil**
	kosher salt and pepper, to taste

Remove peels and seeds from roasted chiles and chop into large pieces. Place chiles, garlic, nuts, and cilantro in a food processor. Pulse until mixture is coarse but evenly minced. Add cheese, cumin, and lime juice.

Drizzle in oil while processing chile mixture to a smooth texture. Start with 1/4 cup olive oil for a thicker paste-like pesto. Add more olive oil if you prefer a runnier texture. Season with salt and pepper. Adjust with more cumin if desired. Store in refrigerator for 3–4 days. Serve with grilled chicken, over pasta, or in potato salad. Makes about 2 cups.

OAXACAN PEANUTS

4	**dried chiles de arbol**
I tablespoon	**vegetable oil**
4 cloves	**garlic,** peeled, finely minced
I can (25 ounces)	**Spanish Peanuts,** with skins
2	**lime wedges**
2 tablespoons	**finely grated lime zest,** (about 2 limes)
I tablespoon	**salt**

Remove the stems and seeds from the chiles; chop. Heat oil in a large frying pan over medium-high heat. Add chiles and garlic to pan and stir until garlic is soft and chiles are toasted. Make sure not to burn chiles. Reduce heat to medium-low and add peanuts. Stir constantly until peanuts are completed toasted and skins have darkened, about 7–8 minutes. Remove peanuts from heat, spritz with lime juice, and toss in a bowl with the zest and salt.

Store peanuts in an airtight container in refrigerator for up to I week. Heat before serving. Makes 2 cups.

CHIPOTLE MAYONNAISE

2 cloves	**garlic,** peeled
¾ teaspoon	**salt**
I cup	**mayonnaise**
2 tablespoons	**minced chipotle pepper in adobo**
4 teaspoons	**honey**
¼ teaspoon	**pepper**

Mince garlic on cutting board, sprinkle with some salt, and mash into a paste with the side of a knife or back of a spoon.

In a small bowl, stir together the garlic, mayonnaise, chipotle, honey, pepper, and remaining salt until well combined. Refrigerate for up to 2 weeks in a covered container. Makes I cup.

GARLIC-CHILE OIL

4	**dried guajillo chiles**
2	**dried New Mexico chiles**
1 ½ cups	**light olive or vegetable oil**
1 pinch	**salt and pepper**
5 cloves	**garlic,** peeled, sliced

Remove stem and some seeds from chiles and chop. Toast chile pieces in a dry medium saucepan over medium-high heat until fragrant, making sure not to burn. Add oil, salt and pepper, and heat until oil begins to bubble around chiles. Remove from heat and add garlic. Cover and steep for 1–2 hours. Strain.

Refrigerate for up to 2 weeks. Heat before using. Delicious when used in salad dressing, drizzled on potatoes, brushed on bread, or as a finishing oil with your favorite dishes. Makes 1 ½ cups.

CARNE ASADA MARINADE

4 cloves	**garlic,** peeled
1	**large handful fresh cilantro leaves**
2	**limes,** halved
1	**small orange,** quartered
1	**jalapeno,** stem removed
2 tablespoons	**white vinegar**
1/2 cup	**olive oil**
1 teaspoon	**kosher salt**
1/2 teaspoon	**pepper**

Place garlic, cilantro, limes, orange, jalapeno, vinegar, oil, salt, and pepper in a food processor and pulse to make a paste. Pour into a ziplock bag and store in refrigerator for up to 1 week. Discard if meat has been marinated in mixture. Makes about 2 cups.

RASPBERRY-CHIPOTLE JAM

9 (8 ounces each)	**freezer-safe containers**
4 cups	**fresh raspberries**
5 cups	**sugar**
3	**chipotle peppers in adobo,** seeded, minced
1	**lemon,** zested, juiced
¾ cups	**water**
1 box (1.75 ounces)	**fruit pectin**

Wash containers and rinse with boiling water; dry.

Crush raspberries in a large bowl and measure exactly 3 cups of crushed berries into a separate bowl. Stir sugar, chipotles, and lemon juice and zest into the 3 cups of berries and let stand for 10–15 minutes, stirring often.

In a small saucepan, stir water and pectin together. Bring to a boil. Continue stirring for 1 minute. Pour over fruit mixture and stir until sugar is completely dissolved.

Fill containers with berry mixture, leaving a ½-inch space at the top of each container. Wipe off edges and put on lids. Leave jam on counter for 24 hours. Store in refrigerator for 3 weeks, or freeze for 6–9 months. Makes 8–9 cups.

Note: This jam is very mild. If you want more heat, add an additional chipotle.

JALAPENO-ORANGE VINAIGRETTE

1	**jalapeno,** seeded, chopped
1/2 cup	**fresh orange juice**
1/4 cup	**champagne or sherry vinegar**
2 tablespoons	**honey**
1 tablespoon	**Dijon mustard**
1/2 cup	**vegetable oil**
1 teaspoon	**salt**
1/2 teaspoon	**pepper**

Place 1/2 of chopped jalapeno in blender with remaining ingredients. Puree mixture until smooth.

Taste vinaigrette and add more jalapeno as desired for heat; puree. Store in a covered container in the refrigerator for up to 2 weeks. Shake before serving. Makes 1 1/2 cups.

NOTES

NOTES

METRIC CONVERSION CHART

Volume Measurements		Weight Measurements		Temperature Conversion	
U.S.	Metric	U.S.	Metric	Fahrenheit	Celsius
1 teaspoon	5 ml	½ ounce	15 g	250	120
1 tablespoon	15 ml	1 ounce	30 g	300	150
¼ cup	60 ml	3 ounces	90 g	325	160
⅓ cup	75 ml	4 ounces	115 g	350	180
½ cup	125 ml	8 ounces	225 g	375	190
⅔ cup	150 ml	12 ounces	350 g	400	200
¾ cup	175 ml	1 pound	450 g	425	220
1 cup	250 ml	2¼ pounds	1 kg	450	230

 Check out these "101" favorites
for more tasty recipes:

Apples	**More Bacon**
Bacon	**More Ramen**
BBQ	**More Slow Cooker**
Beer	**Pancake Mix**
Beans	**Peanut Butter**
Blender	**Pickle**
Cake Mix	**Popcorn**
Canned Biscuits	**Potato**
Casserole	**Pudding**
Cheese	**Pumpkin**
Chicken	**Ramen Noodles**
Chocolate	**Rice**
Dutch Oven	**Rotisserie Chicken**
Eggs	**Salad**
Gelatin	**Slow Cooker**
Grits	**Toaster Oven**
Mac & Cheese	**Tortilla**

Each 128 pages, $9.99

Available at bookstores or directly from GIBBS SMITH
1.800.835.4993
www.gibbs-smith.com

ABOUT THE AUTHOR

Sandra Hoopes graduated from culinary school with an added pastry certificate. She enjoys taking cooking classes from great chefs in Phoenix, Santa Fe, and at the Culinary Institute of America in Hyde Park, New York. Sandra is the creator of the popular blog, everydaysouthwest.com, and a coauthor of *200 Appetizers* and *Burritos!*